1994

Computer
Security

TIME LIFE® BOOKS

Other Publications:

For information on and a full description of any of the Time-
Life Books series listed, please call 1-800-621-7026 or write:
Reader Information
Time-Life Customer Service
P.O. Box C-32068
Richmond, Virginia 23261-2068

This volume is one of a series that examines
various aspects of computer technology
and the role computers play in modern life.

COVER
A computer, rendered as a one and a zero to
symbolize the digital nature of the machine,
stands secure behind a protective brick wall.

UNDERSTANDING COMPUTERS

Computer Security

BY THE EDITORS OF TIME-LIFE BOOKS

TIME-LIFE BOOKS, ALEXANDRIA, VIRGINIA

Contents

1

2

3

4

The Information Society at Risk

Companies that manage their payrolls by computer increasingly offer employees the option of having their paychecks deposited directly into a bank account, instead of receiving a printed check and banking it personally. While many workers gratefully accept the service, others mistrust it; they would rather have the money in hand. Perhaps the doubters are simply old-fashioned and prefer the traditional way of being paid. Whatever their reason, they may have a case.

The money is deposited by a telephone message between computers, one instructing another to subtract the sum from the company's account and to add it to the employee's balance. Coded for brevity, the message may be only a line or two and take less than a second to transmit. Depending on how far the message must travel, it is likely to go part of the way along telephone cables and part as a radio signal beamed between microwave-relay towers or even bounced from a communications satellite in orbit 22,240 miles above the earth.

From start to finish, it is a trip fraught with potential hazards. At either end, someone or something might accidentally garble the message so that too little money is sent or the correct amount goes to the wrong account. A breakdown in the system could occur, convincing the originator of the message that it had been received when it had never been sent. The sequence of messages that make up an entire payroll—or an even larger portion of the trillion dollars that change hands electronically each day in the United States—might be intercepted along the way, allowing the eavesdropper at a single stroke to divert a king's ransom to an unauthorized account.

To be sure, traditional payroll methods are vulnerable, too. A light-fingered thief might steal a check from someone's pocket, or a well-organized band of robbers could highjack the armored truck that delivers a cash payroll. But unlike a purloined check, which is soon missed, or the commotion of an armored-truck job, which instantly galvanizes the police, a computer heist occurs silently, at nearly the speed of light. It might go undiscovered for several days, time enough for a clever crook to make a clean getaway. An employee might not know the electronic paycheck is missing until irate phone calls begin coming in from creditors and checks return from the bank marked "INSUFFICIENT FUNDS."

The transfer of vast wealth by computer is certainly reason enough for those in charge of these systems to see that they function as they are supposed to and that they are secure from internal and external assault. But even more is at stake. Credit-rating information, including credit-card numbers, is stored in computers and passed among those with a legitimate need for the information, in much the same way that a payroll is distributed. A credit-card number in the wrong hands, whether intercepted in transmission or plucked directly from the computer where it is stored, is an invitation to fraud. Though the cardholder may be held responsible for only a small fraction of the unexpected purchases that appear on the bill, in the end the public pays, as credit-card companies raise fees to compensate for the losses.

Barriers to keep outsiders away from a computer and its data provide a partial measure of security. Equally important is safeguarding the system and its contents against subversion from within.

All manner of confidential data, from medical records to the names and addresses of advertisers in the personal column of classifieds, are entrusted to computers. Businesses use computers to store trade secrets that, if stolen by competitors, could lead to bankruptcy. Lawyers store the confidences of their clients in them. Libraries catalogue collections with them. Nations conduct sensitive diplomacy through them and keep secret military plans in them.

Moreover, the flow of daily life depends on computers running without a hitch. They are used to switch electric power from areas that have a surplus to sectors where demand exceeds supply. They coordinate the flow of transcontinental telephone communications. Other computers function in roles where the price of failure or disruption could be catastrophe—the regulation of life-support systems in hospitals, for example, or monitoring of nuclear reactors.

A HOST OF THREATS

From time to time, when computers fail to perform as the world has grown to expect them to, a great hue and cry ensues. But the real wonder is that the remarkable machines function as reliably as they do. Physical hazards abound. Should a careless nudge of an elbow, for example, send a flood of coffee across a desk toward a personal computer, not only the computer is endangered: A magnetic disk used with such computers for storing data could be inundated, and the disk's coffee-coated surface might never again yield up the information entrusted to it. Skin oil and dirt from a fingerprint can have equally unfortunate results on a disk.

A sudden surge or momentary lapse in a computer's electrical power supply is as capable of erasing or scrambling data as the clumsiest data-processing employee or most malicious vandal. Military planners ponder the effects of nuclear explosions on computers and other electronic equipment. Their chief concern is not blast, heat or radiation—usually considered the most devastating forces unleashed by such an explosion—but something called electromagnetic pulse, or EMP. When an atomic or hydrogen bomb detonates, it emits a burst of radiation that interacts with the earth's magnetic field to create a powerful surge of electromagnetic energy. This pulse can induce in the fine web of a computer's circuitry an electrical current strong enough to bring the device to a stop or even destroy it. In that event, missiles could stray off course, aircraft could crash and vital communications could be disrupted.

The human caretakers and taskmasters of computer systems can cause as much harm as any physical hazard. In some instances, these trusted insiders steal or do other deliberate mischief. But more often they make simple mistakes that, taken together, are fully as damaging as crime. "Security seems to be always directed against willful and malicious activities," notes Harry DeMaio, former director of security for International Business Machines, Inc.—yet carelessness is an even larger problem. The inconvenience and financial loss caused by errors and omissions far exceed the toll exacted by crime. For example, lack of diligence in making backup copies of data can transform the annoyance of mistakenly erasing the original into a costly nightmare.

Nonetheless, the most colorful—if not the most destructive—collection of computer nemeses are not professionals who work with computers every day, but youthful amateurs who experiment at night. They are the hackers.

8

That it would be possible one day for even children to violate computers and the information they contain had been foretold by security specialists, who saw that the characteristics that make computers useful and powerful tools also make them attractive and vulnerable targets. Information once stored on paper at scattered locations is now concentrated in large computer data bases and dispersed electronically. Even the speed of computers is a liability: A machine that retrieves facts quickly can also be used to steal facts at a phenomenal rate.

In 1984, editors of *IEEE Spectrum,* a publication of the Institute of Electrical and Electronics Engineers, published an examination of computer security. "Twenty years ago," they wrote, "anyone who committed a crime that involved a computer was probably employed by a data-processing facility." At that time, only government agencies and large corporations had computers, which were run solely by authorized operators. Companies with excess computer capacity sold it to others by means of an arrangement called time sharing, which enables a computer to handle several users or programs at the same time. Within a few years, hundreds of subscribers began communicating great distances with computers over telephone lines specially laid at tremendous cost. To prevent theft of valuable data-processing time by outsiders, subscribers used passwords—secret sequences of letters and numbers—to identify themselves to the computer. But passwords were often compromised, and their illicit use caused legitimate customers to be billed for services they never received.

NETWORK VULNERABILITY
As computers proliferated and companies who owned them wanted their employees to have access to the expensive hardware from a distance, public networks using regular telephone lines to transfer data between computers emerged as an economical substitute for private telephone lines, compounding the security problem. By the 1980s, the IEEE editors continued, "an unauthorized user who had obtained a valid password could get into the computer systems—for profit or for fun—from anywhere in the country."

Even as computers and their lines of communications grew more vulnerable to attack, engineers provided two instruments necessary for youngsters to intrude on them. One is the inexpensive personal computer, the other a device called a modulator/demodulator, or modem, that converts computer data into signals for transmission over telephone lines. Almost before anyone noticed, precocious kids had learned more about computers and how they work than most of the adults who earned a living with them as typists or reservation clerks.

Individuals responsible for computer security, many of them unskilled in the field, by and large did not anticipate an invasion of hackers and were caught unprepared. The passwords of legitimate clients tended to be single words or names easily discovered with a computerized dictionary *(pages 21-25).* Computer specialists at Bell Laboratories in Murray Hill, New Jersey, once showed that they could guess fully half the passwords in use there. Furthermore, passwords were sometimes handed out carelessly, and they were changed too infrequently to guard against compromise. Computer managers failed to remove passwords—easy-to-guess ones like "demo," "system" and "test"—recorded in the machine by manufacturers to aid initial testing and installation. Discovered early on by hackers, they gave easy access to the most advanced equipment.

The term "hacker" may have originated at M.I.T., where students still use it to mean a clever prankster. By the 1960s, it was also applied to classmates who spent their nights in the computer lab, turning out playful programs that included some of the first video games. Hacking later spread from university computer centers to home computers owned by teen-agers. Then some of the fun went sour. By the early 1980s, hackers and hacking had acquired a reputation for reckless maliciousness as a result of widely publicized incidents in which youthful computer enthusiasts infiltrated their way by keyboard and telephone into data banks where they had no business.

• Members of the 414s, a Milwaukee group named after the telephone area code for eastern Wisconsin, were reported to have surreptitiously entered more than 60 computer systems, including ones at Los Alamos National Laboratory in New Mexico, an important United States nuclear-weapons research facility, and Memorial Sloan-Kettering Cancer Center in New York City.

• A Los Angeles high-school student, probing a computer at a state university, gained entry and—"just for the fun of it"—destroyed research data that graduate students had painstakingly assembled and stored in the computer.

• De Paul University in Chicago suffered one computer breakdown after another. Teen-age computer enthusiasts had broken into the system and written a computer program that deleted portions of the operating system, the basic instructions that allow computers to function.

• *Newsweek* reporter Richard Sandza wrote a story about hackers based on messages that he, under the alias Montana Wildhack, had exchanged with them using computer bulletin boards, the electronic equivalent of the cork-and-thumbtack variety. Bulletin boards are maintained by organizations or individuals to enable people to trade information by computer. Sandza's reward: hundreds of harassing telephone calls, death threats, his credit-card numbers traded among hackers across the United States.

THE TOOLS FOR TRESPASSING

The equipment required for such mischief has become no more expensive than a classy skiing outfit or a top-of-the-line bicycle. A few hundred dollars buys a modem and a modest but adequate home computer. With both the computer and a telephone plugged into the modem, electronic trespassing can be remarkably simple. To begin, all a hacker needs is the number of a telephone line hooked up to a computer somewhere. Such numbers may be available for the asking from members of computer clubs; the numbers can also be found posted on computer bulletin boards accessible by modem. The same facility might yield a simple program that tries all the telephone numbers in an exchange, recording the ones that answer with the distinctive voice of a computer. The voice might be that of a computer wired into Telenet, Tymnet, Datapac or Europac, special telephone networks set up for computers to exchange information and programs over. It could be the voice of a bank's computer—or something even more exciting. Breaking into the computer might then require only a few hours of testing likely passwords.

The ease with which hackers gambol among others' computers has gained them considerable notoriety, and deservedly so. Computer hacking, said one college student, "is a game. It is a chance to show you are clever." However, once into a strange computer system, "you need more knowledge than most of these kids possess to do no damage." The 414s purposely deleted the record of their attempts to gain access to Sloan-Kettering's computer in an attempt to erase their tracks. The slight damage they did was easily repaired. But if the group had accidentally deleted patient records, the resulting interruptions of treatment could well have had fatal consequences.

Hackers are often unconcerned with the havoc their computer probing might wreak. As one participant at a hackers' convention near San Francisco put it: "Once the rockets go up, who cares where they come down? That is the hacker ethic, too." Statements from what might be called the radical left among hackers sound even more anarchic. "Philosophically," pronounced Richard Stallman, a self-professed hacker and expert programmer who has placed some of his best work in the public domain, "we don't believe in property rights."

AID FOR THE INSECURE
With computers, data and programs vulnerable not only to hackers but to out-and-out criminals, duplicitous insiders and acts of God, a new industry has sprung up to keep all components safe. There are companies that provide storage for preserving duplicate copies of irreplaceable data, the loss of which has put more than one company out of business. The facilities are as secure against theft as a bank vault—and far superior in the protection they offer against changes in temperature and humidity that can shorten the life of magnetic disks and tapes. New methods are being explored to verify the identity of someone seeking access to a computer and the information it contains. One technique matches the pattern of blood vessels in the retina—as unique as a fingerprint—against a catalogue of individuals' retinal images stored in the computer; similar comparisons are possible using the distinctive tone and timbre of a person's voice or the inimitable outline of a hand (pages 45-57).

Other companies specialize in computers designed to block signals that would otherwise emanate from monitors and keyboards or from deep inside a machine's circuitry and allow an eavesdropper to listen in on the computer's business (pages 94-97). Still other manufacturers produce computers designed to operate flawlessly under extremes of heat, cold and humidity, and even after being run over by a truck. So-called fault-tolerant computers rarely stumble even when something goes awry inside that would bring an ordinary computer to a halt. These computers are much to be desired for such applications as air-traffic control systems, where a sudden shutdown could cause calamity.

Specially designed operating systems—combinations of programs that contain the instructions necessary for a computer to perform fundamental tasks such as retrieving data from storage and moving it around inside the computer—closely monitor the activities of everyone using the system to prevent even those most skilled in manipulating the machine from sneaking a look at any information they are not entitled to see. Confidential messages that must move through communications channels where anyone with the right equipment could intercept them may be encrypted so as to thoroughly garble the contents.

With so many security options to choose from, an army of consultants has arisen. Selling advice about what ought to be protected and the best way to go about doing so, they are most often entrepreneurs who go into business for

Mapping a System's Vulnerabilities

The hardest kind of computer system to protect is one with multiple users, some of whom are connected to the mainframe from remote stations. The typical multi-user system, shown below and on the following two pages, is vulnerable at many points, not unlike a house with numerous doors and windows. The more people and hardware involved, the greater the chance of trouble.

Physical threats to a system represent one broad category of

Local terminals. Housed with the mainframe to which they are wired, local terminals are prime gateways for mischief-minded insiders who may already have legitimate access to the system. Such terminals have no microprocessor of their own. They rely instead on the central processing unit (CPU) of the host mainframe for all operations. (Remote terminals, shown below, may also operate this way.)

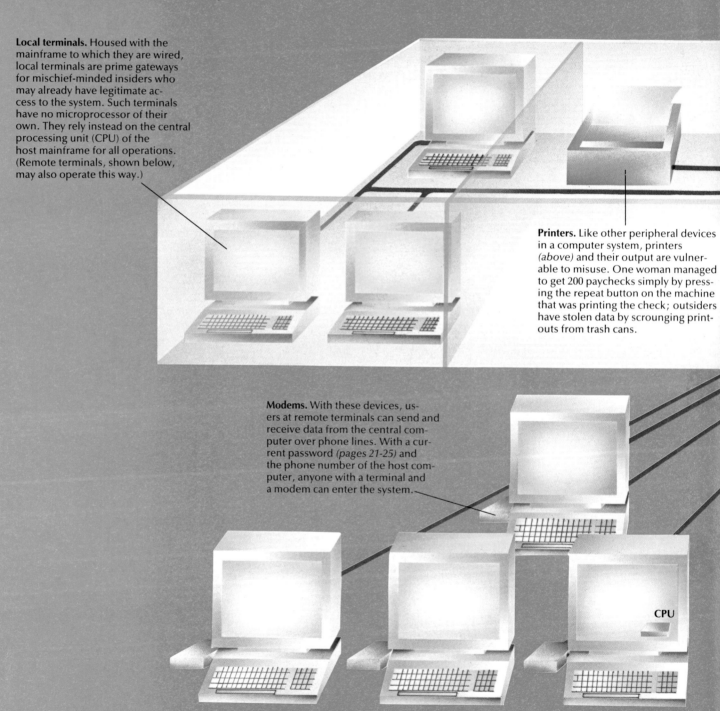

Printers. Like other peripheral devices in a computer system, printers *(above)* and their output are vulnerable to misuse. One woman managed to get 200 paychecks simply by pressing the repeat button on the machine that was printing the check; outsiders have stolen data by scrounging printouts from trash cans.

Modems. With these devices, users at remote terminals can send and receive data from the central computer over phone lines. With a current password *(pages 21-25)* and the phone number of the host computer, anyone with a terminal and a modem can enter the system.

CPU

risk. Surges in electrical power—caused by lightning, for example—can burn out delicate circuitry. The computer system must be protected against flood or fire as well as against the mundane environmental hazards of heat and high humidity, which are capable of interfering with sensitive electronic operations. But more worrisome by far is the physical threat that is posed by humans.

Simple carelessness is one problem: Dropping and damaging a disk pack can render the data stored on it inaccessible; spilling liquid into a keyboard or disk drive can disable its electronics. Sabotage, too, is a possibility. Inside users can take advantage of their ready access to vandalize equipment; outsiders can cut cables or plant bombs. In most cases, however, the aim of those who attempt to breach a computer system's security is not to damage the system itself but to tamper with or steal the information it contains.

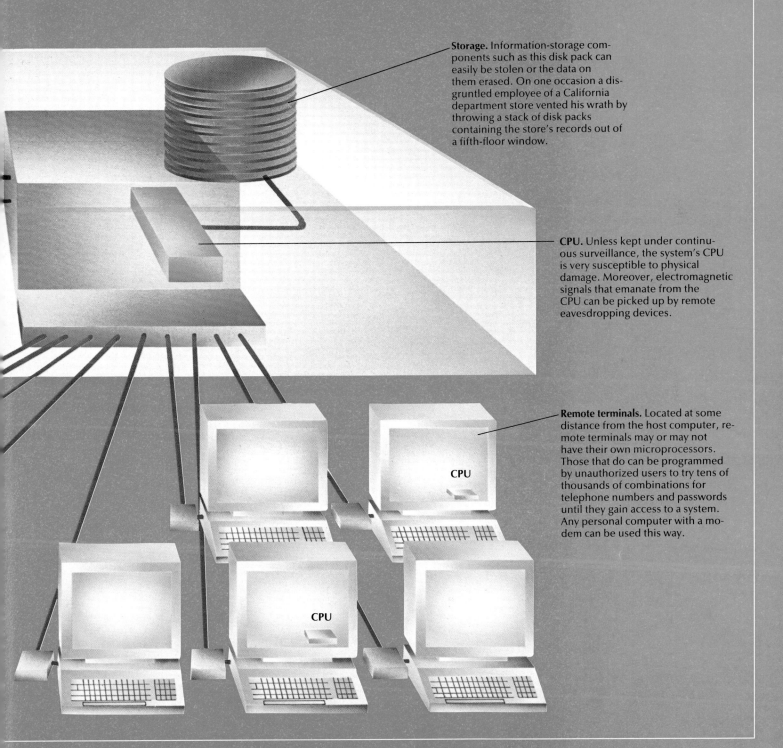

Storage. Information-storage components such as this disk pack can easily be stolen or the data on them erased. On one occasion a disgruntled employee of a California department store vented his wrath by throwing a stack of disk packs containing the store's records out of a fifth-floor window.

CPU. Unless kept under continuous surveillance, the system's CPU is very susceptible to physical damage. Moreover, electromagnetic signals that emanate from the CPU can be picked up by remote eavesdropping devices.

Remote terminals. Located at some distance from the host computer, remote terminals may or may not have their own microprocessors. Those that do can be programmed by unauthorized users to try tens of thousands of combinations for telephone numbers and passwords until they gain access to a system. Any personal computer with a modem can be used this way.

CPU

CPU

The Trespasser's Devious Methods

Once a computer system has been penetrated, the intruder can use the system's own software to pilfer information (and often money as well) and to erase or create data. Such software includes operating systems, the programs that serve to coordinate a computer's internal housekeeping functions; utility programs, which perform tasks such as copying data from one storage medium to another; and application programs, which allow users to do specific jobs such as bookkeeping or word processing.

When not in use, both software and data reside in external storage on disks or tape. To start up a system or get access to a program or data file, a user must bring software and data into the computer's temporary memory—also called random-access memory, or RAM. (Information in RAM disappears when the machine is turned off; so-called read-only memory, or ROM, holds permanent instructions for the machine.)

An intruder intent on tampering with a system's programs and data can do so while this information is en route to or from temporary memory or storage. More often, however, the tampering is done before the information is put into the system. In a practice called data diddling, for instance, students' grades might be altered before they are entered into a school's computerized records.

More difficult to achieve—and to detect—is an invasion known as a trap door. Usually, this involves a programmer's writing into an otherwise secure program a secret sequence of instructions. The program is then put into the system, where it operates normally—but the programmer can invoke the hidden instructions with a special code to gain unauthorized access to restricted parts of the system. A similar ploy, equally difficult to trace, is the time bomb, an instruction that triggers computer action, such as the payment of money or the deletion of incriminating records, at a fixed future date when the perpetrator is far away.

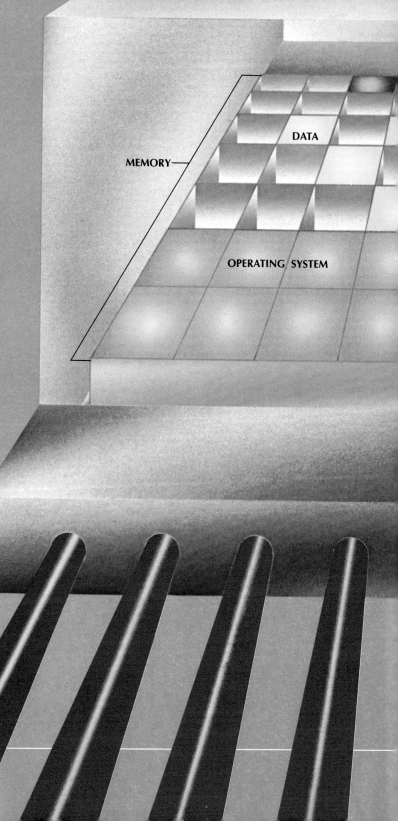

MEMORY

DATA

OPERATING SYSTEM

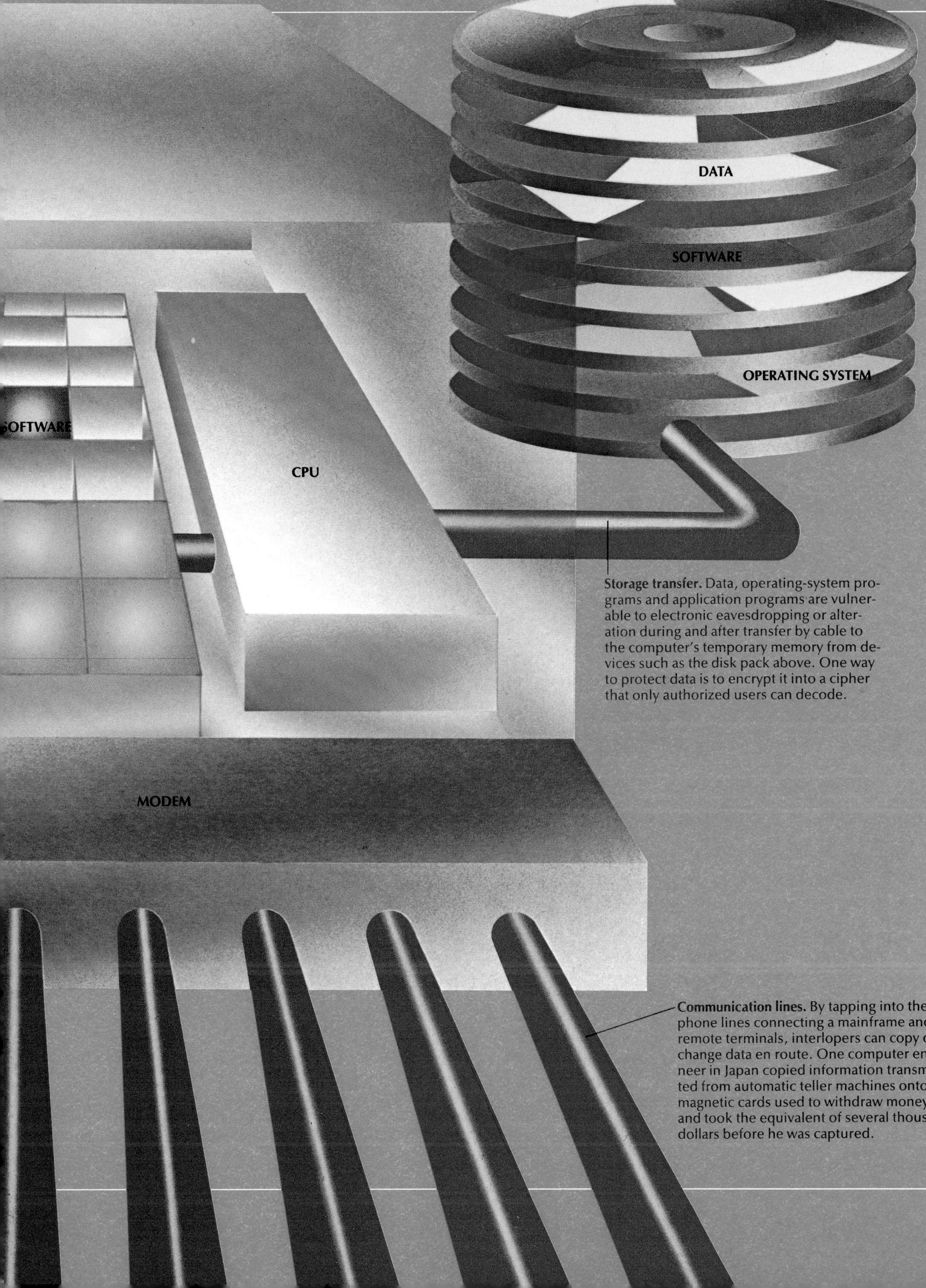

DATA

SOFTWARE

OPERATING SYSTEM

SOFTWARE

CPU

MODEM

Storage transfer. Data, operating-system programs and application programs are vulnerable to electronic eavesdropping or alteration during and after transfer by cable to the computer's temporary memory from devices such as the disk pack above. One way to protect data is to encrypt it into a cipher that only authorized users can decode.

Communication lines. By tapping into the phone lines connecting a mainframe and its remote terminals, interlopers can copy or change data en route. One computer engineer in Japan copied information transmitted from automatic teller machines onto magnetic cards used to withdraw money and took the equivalent of several thousand dollars before he was captured.

themselves after serving in a similar capacity with a large company, the government or the armed forces. Others have come to the profession with years of firsthand experience working the other side of the fence.

Consider John Maxfield. As a child growing up in Michigan in the mid-1950s, Maxfield was intrigued by electronics. At the age of 12, he built a primitive computer. Then, in his teens, he became a "phone phreak," the name given to people who manipulated the telephone system by electronic trickery. Phone phreaks might be considered the original hackers, and John Maxfield was one of the best. Independently of others, he invented both the so-called black box and a successor, the blue box, to avoid paying for long-distance telephone calls.

Wired to the telephone, the black box reduced the voltage used to send a voice over a telephone to a level that was too low to trip the voice-activated switch at the telephone company that controlled billing, but still high enough for the voice to be heard. The blue box had keys that reproduced single-frequency tones available to telephone operators but not to callers from ordinary telephones, which produce double-frequency tones. After dialing a number, pressing the proper sequence of keys before the telephone was answered interrupted the call but kept the line open. Thereafter, any call the phone phreak dialed was seen as originating, not from his own number, but from the number at the other end of the open line, to which the call was billed.

TURNCOAT HACKERS

Maxfield struck a deal with the telephone company: To escape prosecution, he agreed never to reveal the secrets he had discovered. He went on to a modest life in Detroit, installing office telephone systems and repairing teletypewriter equipment. In his spare time he toyed with computers, in 1979 becoming the sysop, or system operator, of the Southwest Michigan Computer Club's electronic bulletin board, one of the first in the United States.

Over the years, Maxfield had reformed to the degree that he was offended by acts of software piracy committed with the aid of the bulletin board. It was not unusual to see copyrighted computer games—which, to the bulletin board, are merely long and complicated messages—illegally posted there, free for the taking by any club member. After learning of an FBI inquiry into the theft of such games, he offered his services in running to ground not only game pirates but phone phreaks and anyone else he could discover illegally touring the nation's computer systems. The government eagerly accepted.

"In a way," he said later, "it was the ultimate hacker challenge, to hack the hackers." Granted federal authority to phreak, Maxfield became known on hacker bulletin boards as Cable Pair, an accommodating fellow, eager to explain to those he took into his confidence everything he knew about computers and phreaking. Whenever he learned the identity of a lawless correspondent, he would turn the facts over to the FBI for action. "I've lost track of the number of people," he said. "I count as one of my 'kills' anyone I've provided information on who was subsequently arrested."

Cable Pair operated for 18 months or so before he unintentionally compromised his own identity: He took his evidence directly to a business victimized by hackers instead of going through his FBI contact, and word of his true role soon leaked to the hacker underworld. His cover blown, Maxfield became the target of other hackers bent on getting even. The harassment compelled him to change his telephone number several times, a practice that severely disrupted his teletype-writer repair business. So he switched careers and founded Board Scan to keep tabs on hacker bulletin boards, reporting to credit-card and telephone companies any customer account numbers that he found there. "It was dirty business," Maxfield recalled of his days as Cable Pair, "but I don't think the hackers can be allowed to continue, because if they do, they will ultimately bring us all down."

MORE BARK THAN BITE
Security consultant Robert Courtney, formerly of IBM, has asserted that, for all the furor surrounding hackers, they "have done less damage to corporate computer systems than overflowing lavatories." Moreover, they have not even come close to breaching the security of computers, such as the ones at the North American Aerospace Defense Command (NORAD), that manage the defenses of the United States. Nor are they likely to: Such computers are linked to no public network that might let a hacker enter, and they are well secured against physical trespass (pages 36-39). One frequent member of the "Tiger Teams" that test the vulnerability of computer systems has commented, "I do not know any way even remotely possible of getting into those computers without a breach of trust."

The security of other computer networks, some of which may carry confidential research data, can be improved by the addition of such devices as dial-back machines. After confirming the identity of the person seeking access by modem, a dial-back box hangs up. It then dials the number authorized for that person to verify that a stranger is not trying to hack into the system from a different location. Not every computer is worthy of such measures. For example, the Los Alamos computer that the 414s broke into contained no secrets; it was being used mainly to experiment with computer mail systems.

Genuine criminals intent on theft or destruction are no more difficult than hackers to keep at bay. Donn Parker, an investigator of the illegal use of computers who is based at the research organization SRI International, once remarked that only rarely do "we get a crime in which somebody has done something intelligent, and it makes our day." Most of the cases that come to light are, in his view, disappointingly unsophisticated and depend primarily on the kind of simple laxity that hackers exploit.

In 1978, a man named Stanley Rifkin stole $10.2 million dollars from a Los Angeles bank simply by posing as a consultant hired to improve the operation of the bank's communications center, where computer messages for transferring funds originate. By interviewing console operators there, he collected all the computer passwords and bank codes necessary to pose as an officer of the institution over the phone and have the funds transferred to a New York bank account and thence to Switzerland. He was apprehended—and sentenced to eight years in prison—only because he bragged about the caper to his lawyer, trusting that his attorney would not report the crime because of the confidential relationship between attorney and client. Unable to tolerate such an abuse, the lawyer turned his client in to the FBI.

A Bell Labs security expert was once asked to help a company protect its data. After an interview with an officer of the firm, he happened past a room labeled Message Center. "I walked around the room unescorted, with no badge or identification," he recalled. "I looked at each terminal. I spent ten or fifteen minutes there and no one asked me who I was," ample time to learn all he needed to break into the organization's computers.

Gaps in security like that one can be plugged simply by keeping a door locked; Stanley Rifkin would have been thwarted had anyone asked him for identification. It is more difficult to prevent crimes by those who have the key to the lock or who have valid identification. They need not break into the system; they are already inside. And there they might become so-called data diddlers, altering the information held by the computer to their own advantage. For example, according to a British science periodical, most of the computer crimes reported in Great Britain involve false information put into a computer: "These frauds are the same in essence as any other kind of embezzlement. They take advantage of gaps in an accounting system and depend on the criminal knowing he will not be quickly discovered."

In 1980, such a crime took place in Baltimore. A Social Security clerk, Janet Braintree Blair, observed that new applicants sometimes were paid a smaller lump sum than they were entitled to when they began to collect benefits. Unlike the recipients, Blair understood precisely how the lump sum was calculated. When she came upon one that was incorrect, she requested a check from the computer for the additional funds, replacing the rightful payee's name and address with her own. The next morning, she restored the original address. Blair mailed herself no less than $108,000 in fraudulent Social Security checks before being caught and convicted for her embezzlement.

LARCENY AT THE TOP

High officials of an organization can use computers to defraud the public on a scale never before possible, as was revealed in 1973 with the Equity Funding Corporation, which passed itself off as a multimillion-dollar insurance and financial conglomerate. In that instance, the president of the company and several of his underlings issued 64,000 bogus insurance policies. Taken together, the policies that an insurance company issues present a distinctive profile based on such factors as amounts of coverage, size of premiums, and numbers of policies canceled and benefits paid. By using the computer to make certain that, as a group, the false policies were indistinguishable in these and other important characteristics from the company's legitimate policies, the perpetrators of the fraud concealed it for 10 years. When the ruse eventually was exposed, Equity Funding went under, leaving 7,000 investors holding worthless stock and more than 50 lawsuits to be settled in the wake of the disaster.

For the Equity Funding fraud to succeed for as long as it did required the collusion of a handful of computer programmers in the actuarial department, where insurance risks are calculated. They were the ones who made certain that the bogus policies mimicked the real ones closely enough to avert detection. Programmers like these, who have been granted access to the very heart of the computer, present the greatest danger. With their savvy, they can subvert computer systems in ways that may never be detected.

Among their weapons are Trojan horses, logic bombs and viruses. A Trojan horse is a program that, like the gift that doomed ancient Troy, conceals agents of ruin; they operate invisibly whenever the program is invoked, stealing data, passwords or worse. An expert programmer can write a Trojan horse that is invisible to any but the most detailed investigation. Logic bombs are set to go off at a future time or event. For example, a programmer might write a logic bomb to wreak revenge if the programmer were ever dismissed. A program of a few lines, secreted away among the tens of thousands of instructions that constitute a computer operating system, could command the computer to remove every employee from the payroll if one particular name were ever deleted. Viruses, as the name suggests, are infectious, data-gobbling programs that spread like plague, either on floppy-disk "carriers" or through networks connecting more than one computer (Chapter 3).

Some experts play down the threat posed by computer programmers. "Contrary to all the publicity," Robert Courtney has asserted, "we really do not have a technical security problem." By his count, only seven of a thousand computer break-ins reported over a recent four-year period were the work of professional programmers. "In five of the seven cases, the programmers stole money just by using the system as it was designed to be used, while in the other two, programmers carried out robberies by modifying existing programs illegally."

ASSESSING THE DAMAGE
The multitude of chinks in computer armor add up to substantial potential for harm worldwide, whoever the perpetrators might be. A South American bank reportedly lost $13 million in a fraud that was not discovered until six months after the event. In Milan, Italy, several bank employees transferred large sums from customers' computerized accounts to their own. In a single year, Japan reported 472 fraudulent transactions involving automatic teller machines.

Some computer-security authorities do not believe that an undiscovered swamp of computer crime lies in wait. Others, with comparable credentials, contend that unreported crimes far outnumber those that come to light. They point out that clever crimes may never be discovered. And should they be, the victims—especially banks and large corporations—may decline to prosecute. According to Robert Courtney, "Shareholders, voters and policyholders all look on major fraud as evidence of gross mismanagement, and usually they are right. If a company decides to prosecute, the crime gets into the newspapers. This means that the bigger the crime, the lower the probability that it will be prosecuted." Following this line of reasoning, estimates of the monetary damages vary so widely that they qualify as little more than wild guesses. In England, The Daily Telegraph calculated that computer-related frauds cost British industry "between 500 million and 2.5 billion pounds a year." In the United States, the figure ranges from $300 million to $5 billion.

Legal remedies for at least some of these depredations began appearing in the United States and Europe in the late 1970s. By the end of the 1980s in America, for example, new federal and state laws were being used to convict scores of computer bandits of a broad array of electronic crimes, from theft, fraud and extortion to unauthorized access, the computer equivalent of trespassing. Depending on the offense, penalties range from modest fines through forfeiture of the computer equipment used to commit illegal acts to 10-year prison terms. Despite the growth of computer-crime legislation, however, the prosecution of such escapades remains a challenge. Perpetrators in some cases are minors, invoking the full legal apparatus that protects juvenile offenders. Seemingly criminal actions—the writing of certain viruses, for example—may sidestep the letter of existing laws. Moreover, a crime might begin at a computer in one state, ravage a computer in another and spirit the booty to yet another state or even to a foreign country. Questions arise: Where was the crime committed? Who has jurisdiction in prosecuting it?

Such difficulties are probably no more than the legal growing pains incurred as the justice system adapts to a new arena of crime. Even so, legislation alone will no more likely end computer crime than laws against breaking and entering have stopped burglary. City dwellers and suburbanites bolt doors and windows to protect their possessions; managers of computer systems must take similar measures to keep out thieves, vandals and curious kids.

THE PRICE OF COMPUTER SECURITY

The cost of denying such miscreants entry to computer systems is one reason why, with few exceptions outside the military and the national defense industry, computer security has received all too little attention. There is the price that one might expect to pay for the tools of security: equipment ranging from locks on doors to computerized gate-keepers that stand watch against hackers, special software that prevents employees from peeking at data that is none of their concern *(pages 73-85)*, a staff trained to be alert for people seeking unauthorized access. The bill can range from hundreds of dollars to many thousands, depending on the degree of assurance sought.

But there is also a hidden price, one paid in time and inconvenience. Often, new work rules must be imposed, disrupting the old way of doing things. No longer can identifying passwords be easy-to-remember birthdates and nicknames, nor can their less-memorable replacements be posted at the computer for ready reference. The process of encoding and decoding data slows the computer, as well as the progress of workers who may already be saddled with impossible deadlines. Clip-on badges, which wrinkle blouses and shirts, may be found necessary to control access to a computer room. Such complications inhibit the adoption of effective computer-security measures.

It may even be necessary to make the computer less "friendly," in the vernacular of data processing. If gaining access to a computer is easy for those authorized to do so, the process may offer few obstacles to a determined outsider trying to get in. A computer system that teaches insiders how to use it, for example, can offer the same assistance to unauthorized people.

Managers of computer systems can find it perplexing to decide what information ought to be protected and to what length they should pursue the matter. No combination of technologies promises unbreachable security. Experts in the field agree that someone with sufficient resources can crack almost any computer defense. And the attack need not be direct. For example, it may cost a criminal far less in time and money to bribe a disloyal employee for the key that deciphers a company's encrypted messages than to assemble the computer power needed to crack the code. In the end, everyone who works with computers bears a measure of responsibility for their security, whether it is to decide what measures should be taken to maintain those safeguards or simply not to betray them.

Turning Away
an Attack
with a Word

Passwords are a multi-user computer system's usual first line of defense against intrusion. A password may be any combination of alphabetic and numeric characters, to a maximum length set by the particular system. Many systems can accommodate passwords up to 40 characters long; some can handle as many as 80 characters. Would-be users are not allowed into the system until they confirm their identity and access rights by keying in the password that matches the one on file with their name.

Since even legitimate users may make typing mistakes, many systems allow a minute for three to five tries before refusing access or breaking the telephone connection. Unless the system has security methods sophisticated enough to detect repeated entry attempts from the same terminal, an unauthorized person is free to try again at will. Outside hackers who have found (or guessed) at least the name of a legitimate user can thus program their own computers not only to dial the target system repeatedly but also, in an approach known as a brute-force attack, to keep trying different combinations of characters in the hope of hitting upon a password that works.

Ideally, then, a password should be constructed so as to withstand a brute-force attack long enough to make it not worth the hacker's time. To this end, multi-user systems often have a security officer who periodically assigns every user a pronounceable but random password generated by computer. The longer the password, the more possibilities a hacker's password-guessing program must work through.

The catch is that a long, randomly generated password can also be difficult to remember, tempting a user to write it down, which immediately makes it a security risk. But passwords that are easy to remember—a mother's first name, say, or a significant word—are susceptible to discovery for other reasons, chief among them being that they are gathered into handy sources such as dictionaries. With a dictionary of 2,000 common names, for instance, a hacker would be able to find a first name, even a long one, in an average of five hours of repeated tries.

On the following pages, a metaphorical computer-as-fortress is used to illustrate the relative security of random and meaningful passwords. The best compromise, of course, is a password that is as difficult to discover as a random assortment, but has a nonrandom meaning known only to its owner.

The Pros and Cons of Randomness

In this analogy of a computer system as a fortress, the password is composed of 10 characters—ATA02CTW08—each selected from 36 alphanumeric possibilities at each of the fort's 10 tiers. An attacker would have to find the correct combination to align the characters vertically and unlock the drawbridge. Even a computer that enabled the attacker to test one million guesses per second—a power far in excess of the personal-computer systems typically available to hackers—would require, on average, close to 60 years to ferret out a random 10-character password from the 3,700,000,000,000,000 possible combinations.

Random passwords. As the chart below demonstrates, increasing the length of a random password can make it drastically more difficult to discover. With each additional character, both the number of possible combinations and the average time required to find the password increase exponentially. However, passwords made up of truly random combinations are harder to remember the longer they get.

Number of Characters	Possible Combinations	Average Time to Discover
1	36	6 minutes
2	1,300	4 hours
3	47,000	5 days
4	1,700,000	6 months
5	60,000,000	19 years
6	2,000,000,000	630 years
7	78,000,000,000	25,000 years
8	2,800,000,000,000	890,000 years
9	100,000,000,000,000	32,000,000 years
10	3,700,000,000,000,000	1,200,000,000 years

The Varying Security of Memorable Words

The alternative to a randomly generated password is one chosen because it is easy to remember—a set of initials, for instance, or the name of a favorite aunt. The key to the security of such a mnemonic device is not its length per se but whether it can be found in a relatively small, ready-made source such as a name dictionary. The password for the fortress shown here is the same length—10 characters—as the password on page 22, but this one is the word "instrument." A hacker using word-processor software designed to check the spelling of 60,000 words can find a word from that list in an average of only seven days.

The best mnemonic devices combine the advantage of easy recall with the security of randomness. A familiar phrase or line of poetry, for instance, can be compressed to form a combination of letters that would never appear in a dictionary. Similarly, the password on page 22 looks like a meaningless jumble, but in fact it is composed of the initials and birth months of the user's two grandmothers—a combination particularly easy for the user to remember.

Mnemonic passwords. As shown below, so long as the mnemonic password is not a common name or a real word, security increases with length. The greater the number of possibilities a hacker must sort through, the better the chances of a password's remaining undiscovered.

How Chosen	Example	Number of Possibilities	Average Time to Discover
Name (short/long)	Al/Charlotte	2,000 (name dictionary)	5 hours
Word (short/long)	a/photoduplication	60,000 (spelling checker)	7 days
Two words together	dogcat	3,600,000,000	1,140 years
Mix of initials and significant dates	ATA02CTW08	3,700,000,000,000,000	1,200,000,000 years
First line of a poem	Maryhadalittlelamb	10,000,000,000,000,000,000,000,000,000	3,000,000,000,000,000,000,000,000 years
First two letters of each word of a poem's first line	Mahaalila	100,000,000,000,000	32,000,000 years

Warding Off Physical Perils

Perpetrators of computer-related crimes, like other kinds of criminals, often seek a degree of anonymity after they have been found out, even though their cases are a matter of public record. So it is with a former computer-operations supervisor for Imperial Chemical Industries (ICI) who, preferring to keep his name to himself, goes by the pseudonym Jon. As Jon recounted his story some time later, his caper began innocently enough. Eager to tighten computer security at Imperial Chemical's installations in the Netherlands, he was reading a book on the subject when he came across an account of valuable computer tapes that had been stolen and held for ransom.

Jon was intrigued by this crime; he, too, had access to tapes and disks, ones that contained key records of the London-based multinational's extensive European operations. He discussed the case with a colleague, a computer-systems analyst at Imperial, and during idle moments, the two men fantasized about pulling off a "kidnapping" like the one described in the book.

Soon thereafter, when Jon was passed over for promotion, greed and disgruntlement brought the fantasy to life. On a quiet Saturday in 1977, he drove his car to two different company installations and simply signed out the data tapes and disks, as he was authorized to do. He and his systems-analyst colleague, whom he had enlisted as an accomplice, now had in their possession 48 sets of disks and 54 tapes—the originals plus the backup, or duplicate, copies, which had been stored at the second site. The two thieves stashed the purloined files in a rented garage.

For the return of the data to ICI, the men demanded a ransom of £275,000—nearly $500,000—to be delivered in London. This appraisal of the stolen data's value was a conservative one; the files contained vital information such as payroll records and pension-fund investments, as well as accounts payable and receivable. Officials of Imperial Chemical estimated that if the missing data could not be recovered, the company would have to spend two million pounds to reconstruct the information and would lose a like amount in revenues. To demonstrate to ICI what would happen to the hostage data if the company did not comply promptly with the ransom demand, the two thieves sent along a partially erased backup tape.

Imperial Chemical Industries capitulated. At the appointed hour, an ICI representative appeared at the rendezvous in Piccadilly Circus, the center of London's hustle and bustle, carrying a black briefcase stuffed with ransom money in £5 and £10 notes. As instructed, he stood on the curb and, feeling rather foolish, held out the briefcase at arm's length. The two extortionists roared up on a motorcycle and lurched to a stop. As one of them reached for the loot, they received instead a rude greeting. ICI had tipped off Scotland Yard, and 10 London bobbies, disguised as street sweepers, collared the none-too-clever kidnappers and packed them off to jail.

The affair had a happy ending for ICI, which got its precious data back from

From bolts of lightning to seemingly inconsequential specks of dust, physical hazards to computers abound. Prudent measures should be taken against the most threatening, but the best insurance is to store duplicate copies of data—and even a spare computer—in a safe place in case of disaster.

the police right away. Under similar circumstances, one United States accounting firm was less fortunate. Although the authorities nabbed the employee who had attempted to extort $100,000 from the company after making off with a valuable set of computer programs, the county sheriff—unlike Scotland Yard—failed to grasp the firm's urgent need for the software. He impounded the programs as evidence, then refused to allow the company access to them. In desperation, the organization's president committed a computer crime of his own. Late one night he broke into the sheriff's office, took the programs to a data center, where he copied them, and then, in a burglary in reverse, returned the originals to the evidence pound.

THE COST OF INDIFFERENCE

The very idea of programs and data being held for ransom as if they were a millionaire's children or priceless jewels illustrates the special security problems posed by computer systems. On one level, these systems may be considered merely high-tech office equipment. But the potential for loss dwarfs the impact that stolen typewriters or even a fire-ravaged office can have on a company or a government agency. The cost of replacing all the noncomputer office equipment of a large organization does not approach the price, often measured in the millions of dollars, of a new computer system and its attendant software.

Clearly, a company or agency bent upon making its computer system physically safe confronts a bewildering array of threats. A well-planned theft, a terrorist's bomb or a vengeful employee in the computer room exacts one kind of toll. But money is also lost and public confidence in computers diminished whenever something as mundane as a burst water pipe disrupts the fragile structures of electronic circuitry and magnetically stored information that increasingly honeycomb modern society. Joel S. Zimmerman, founder of a security consulting firm in Virginia, has written that computer systems cannot be protected against everything: "The tension in computer security comes from making choices—what will be controlled and what will not."

A formal risk analysis can help those who are responsible for the decisions. This widely recommended procedure, which is also used to evaluate the threat from hackers and others whose weapon against computers is the computer itself, attempts to foresee the consequences of a failure in security. Among other things, risk analysis considers the value of the assets to be protected, including the costs of disruption, the nature and probability of potential threats, and the price of proposed safeguards. When the evaluation is complete, risk analysis guides computer managers toward the threats and vulnerabilities they should address first in order to get the most protection from the always limited amount of money at their disposal for security.

Most experts warn that recommendations produced by risk analysis are no more than educated guesses at the very best. Estimating the probability of a fire, explosion or burglary can scarcely be described as an exact science. Moreover, the likelihood of some events, such as one that occurred during the maiden flight of the space shuttle *Atlantis* in 1985, is so small as to be unimaginable. Less than five minutes before the shuttle was due to pass over a satellite-tracking station in Senegal, the station experienced a momentary—but alarming—fluctuation in power. A frantic search for the cause unearthed a slightly scorched

18-inch monitor lizard that was lodged in a tangle of power cables. Operators persuaded the creature to abandon its shocking nest by poking at it with a screwdriver, and the station proceeded to track *Atlantis'* flight over Senegal without further reptilian interference.

Trying to make accurate predictions based on highly uncertain information leads more often than not to meaningless results, an argument sometimes used against conducting formal risk analysis. Cost is another deterrent. Even with the aid of special software packages designed for the purpose, risk analysis is a time-consuming process and therefore almost always expensive. Adolph Cecula, head of computer security at the U.S. Geological Survey, once calculated what it would cost to perform risk analyses of that agency's more than 1,700 computers: upward of six million dollars.

Some critics of risk analysis question its emphasis on cost-effectiveness. The idea that one should not spend $200,000 to protect against $100,000 in potential losses seems to make sense on the surface—especially if the possibility of such a loss is remote. But this approach often fails to account for other factors, such as the public perception of the reliability of a data-processing system. Banks, health-care facilities and other institutions where breakdowns might jeopardize people's welfare and even their lives must have absolute confidence that, short of Armageddon, computers will keep operating.

While risk analysis draws its share of critics, few would abandon the process entirely, agreeing that making sensible security choices requires exhaustive consideration of the potential threats. There are two major categories of dangers: hazards of the environment and those posed by people. Security experts typically begin with the first group.

MAINTAINING A TEMPERATE CLIMATE

Environmental problems include not only events that directly imperil the computer system itself but also breakdowns in its supporting equipment. Smoothly functioning air conditioning, for example, is of critical importance to the uninterrupted operation of a computer system. Before the advent of sealed storage drives, computer systems depended on air conditioners to screen out dust particles that could abrade the magnetic surfaces of tapes and disks, causing partial loss of data or even making an entire disk unreadable. Today, the machines are still needed to maintain proper levels of humidity and prevent condensation on delicate mechanisms. Perhaps more important, they cool electronic circuitry, which generates so much heat that a big computer can actually warm an unheated room in winter. Malfunctioning cooling systems have shut down the computers serving a major stock exchange and suspended an airline's reservation service. The resulting revenue loss in each instance amounted to millions of dollars for every day the air conditioners were out of operation.

Unfortunately, cool, dry air can aggravate a phenomenon familiar in wintertime to anyone with nylon carpeting—static electricity. The crackling discharge that is mildly irritating to humans can zap the microchips inside any size of computer, from a desktop model to one that fills a room, with a jolt potent enough to paralyze the machine temporarily and even damage it permanently. Two innovations have helped alleviate this hazard. One solution was the development of a special kind of carpeting that has fine copper wires in the weave. The conductive filaments serve to dissipate static electricity before it can build to a spark. The other solution resides in the computer itself; most modern machines are built to shrug off the average jolt of static electricity by routing it safely past sensitive components.

For the most part, the climate inside a computer facility is under the control of the men and women who manage that facility. But the electrical power that sustains computers can, at times, be so capricious that it may appear to be out of control altogether. Unpredictable fluctuations in the normal power supply often cause trouble that has nothing to do with wayward lizards. These surges and sags,

Cards to Fight Forgery and Fraud

Locks and keys are a traditional way to limit access to secure areas. But keys have a way of getting stolen or copied. The people concerned with the security of computer systems have thus looked for ways to render keylike devices ineffective if they fall into the wrong hands. Some installations combine coded card-keys with passwords. The use of card-keys prevents an intruder from simply guessing at valid passwords, and the password system keeps a thief from gaining access with a card that has been lost but not yet missed.

Three types of card-keys are illustrated here. Each can employ an identifying number or password that is encoded in the card itself, and all are produced by techniques beyond the reach of the average computer criminal. One card makes use of a patented manufacturing process called watermark magnetics, inspired by the watermarks on paper currency. A 12-digit number built into the card's magnetic strip during manufacture cannot be counterfeited.

The other two cards have the capability of storing thousands of times more data than the roughly 2,000 bits contained in a magnetic strip. In optical memory cards (OMCs), data is encoded in one of two ways: by a photolithographic process during manufacture (in which case it is impossible for the card's owner to alter the information) or by a special low-powered laser device purchased by the user. In either case, the data takes the form of coded pits in the surface of the card, which is read by an optical scanner.

Smart cards contain a microchip that is, in effect, a small computer with enough memory to hold both programs and data. The read-only memory holds the card's operating system, and the random-access memory holds temporary results of computations (it does not retain information when the card is disconnected from a power source). In addition, the chip contains a programmable read-only memory that may be altered only under special conditions.

A magnetic watermark. During manufacture of the tape, magnetic particles used to encode the card's permanent identification number are set in zones of varying width at alternating 45-degree angles to the tape's longitudinal axis. Data may then be encoded on the tape, but the identifying structure of the tape itself cannot be altered or copied. A card reader with a special head and circuitry is needed to scan the watermark. ⎯⎯⎯⎯

Optical memory card (OMC). Minute dots representing binary zeros and ones are either photographically etched onto the storage strip during manufacture or burned in later with a tiny, low-powered laser beam. The card, which can hold the equivalent of a 400-page book in its 3¼-by-½-inch strip, is sealed with a protective layer that cannot be removed without destroying the data and invalidating the card. ⎯⎯

Smart card. The card's penny-size microchip contains a processor and three types of memory, totaling 21,800 bits, for storing programs and data. Sensitive information, such as the cardholder's password, is kept in the so-called secret zone of the card's programmable read-only memory; this zone is encoded during manufacture and is not accessible even to the card's owner. ⎯⎯⎯⎯

known as transients, sometimes trigger logic errors that cause programs to go awry or data stored within a computer to be changed inadvertently. In extreme instances, a surge can burn out computer circuitry.

If the power stumbles for as little as $1/100$ of a second, data stored in the machine's temporary memory can be lost. In older systems, a longer power loss may cause a disk drive's record-and-playback heads, which transfer information from computer to disk and back, to crash on the disk's fragile magnetic surface. Under normal conditions, a record-and-playback head never touches the surface of the disk. Instead, it floats about $1/100$ of an inch above the disk, supported on

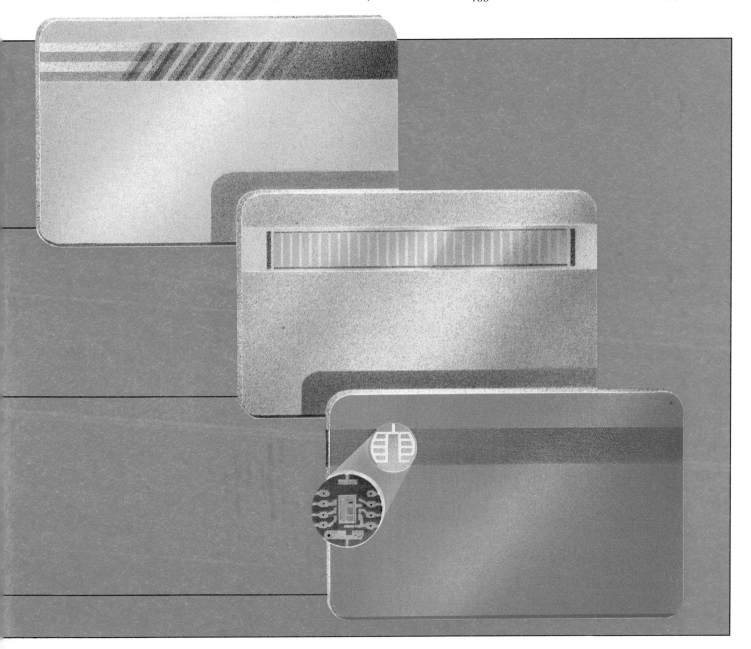

a current of air created by the disk's spinning below the head at high speed. A head crash, as it is known in the trade, gouges the disk and eradicates data recorded there. To prevent this catastrophe, some disk drives are made so that they will retract their heads at the first flicker in the power supply.

Transients occur routinely when electrical equipment stops or starts anywhere along the power line. As a rule, though, only machinery that consumes large amounts of electricity will produce noticeable effects. For example, when an air-conditioner compressor cycles off or an elevator comes to a stop to discharge or take on passengers, the sharp change in voltage can affect the power supply to nearby computers.

On rare occasions, a conglomeration of small devices can cause similar difficulties. Problems with a computer system in Southend, England, were traced to voltage surges occurring precisely at 10:30 p.m., the end of the television broadcast day and the time when many residents of the city switched off their television sets almost in unison.

During a violent thunderstorm, lightning that surges through power lines can fry a computer's innards or perform other evil deeds. At a computer center in Los Angeles during one such storm, lightning missed the machines but somehow passed through the metal shelving in the data library, generating a magnetic field of such strength that it erased information worth millions of dollars from tapes archived there.

DEFENDING AGAINST TRANSIENTS
Protection from the sometimes disastrous effects of electrical surges and sags is available through a variety of devices. For small machines, some of which consume no more power than a 250-watt light bulb, a surge suppressor or voltage regulator is adequate defense against power transients and costs little. Surge suppressors function by diverting sudden power increases before they peak. Voltage regulators for computers perform the same service and, in addition, fill in voltage dips before they become deep enough to affect the computer. But these devices have too little capacity to work for most large computers, which, together with disk drives and other equipment, burn power at many times the rate of desktop models. Such a system is commonly protected by a motor-generator set, which effectively isolates the computer from brief, random ups and downs in the power supply. To do so, an electric motor uses electricity from the power company to run a generator, which in turn creates new, smoothly flowing electricity for the computer.

However, surge suppressors, voltage regulators and motor-generator sets cannot save a computer from a total power failure, even one that lasts for only a fraction of a second. Salvation in that event is offered by a so-called UPS, or uninterruptible power supply. A UPS system is made up of a complex of electrical apparatus that is built around storage batteries; it not only filters out transients but provides instantaneous backup power during a blackout. The batteries do run down, of course, but they can sustain computers long enough either to shut down the system in an orderly fashion (without loss of data) or to crank up an auxiliary power supply.

Auxiliary power can be expensive. Multiple diesel generators and a roomful of switching equipment to connect them to the computers can raise the cost of backing up a large UPS system, consisting of hundreds of storage batteries, to as much as one million dollars. On the other hand, UPS systems for personal computers can be purchased for a few hundred dollars. But there is no comparably economical backup generator. Small gasoline-powered generators, which some homeowners use to run appliances during power failures, are not up to the job.

The shortcomings of such systems were demonstrated by Erik Sandberg-Diment, computer columnist for *The New York Times,* when he plugged a small computer into a 1,200-watt home generator during the blackout imposed on parts of the United States' East Coast by Hurricane Gloria in the autumn of 1985. "Although 1,200 watts is more than enough power to run a personal computer," he wrote afterward, "the quality of current produced by such a putt-putt is simply not refined enough to suit microelectronics. As an experiment, I powered up an old Commodore 64, which promptly acted as if it had lost its mind, its video display turning into snow after a few seconds."

TRIAL BY CONFLAGRATION

As inconvenient and disruptive as power-supply problems may be, they are simple—if sometimes expensive—to solve. But fire, which can flare up outside a computer facility and spread to engulf it, has so many causes that defending against all of them is an impractical goal. When fire rampages through a computer center, it can make the damage caused by a power failure seem trifling.

At the Pentagon, the U.S. military's sprawling headquarters near Washington, D.C., a 300-watt light bulb once was left burning inside a vault where computer tapes were stored. After a time, the bulb had generated so much heat that the ceiling began to smolder. When the door was opened, air rushing into the room brought the fire to life. Before the flames could be extinguished, they had spread to consume three computer systems worth a total of $6.3 million.

The loss of computing capacity in a fire can be far more costly than equipment damage alone. In May 1988, for instance, fire at a computerized Illinois Bell switching station near Chicago deprived tens of thousands of customers of telephone service for several weeks, costing local businesses more than half a billion dollars in lost revenues.

Fire is always near the top of any risk analysis. Whether accidental or not, fires do more damage to computers than almost any other environmental hazard. A study of computer disasters in the United Kingdom confirmed that fire—and its cousin, explosion—accounted for nearly half of the cases surveyed.

Heat is but one component of the threat. Particles of smoke and soot attack the magnetic surfaces of tapes and disks and may continue to work further mischief well after the crisis has passed. In Washington State, volcanic ash from Mount Saint Helens's explosive eruption in 1980 ground away data from disk surfaces and ruined delicate disk-drive mechanisms.

Water used to fight a fire can do as much harm as the flames. Water is poison to a computer that is running. Even a small amount of the liquid may cause short circuits that make a computer go haywire, shut it down completely or ruin it permanently. In 1980, an automatic sprinkler system installed at the U.S. Bureau of the Census malfunctioned and turned itself on in the absence of flames or smoke. A fine spray drenched the bureau's computers, and 19 days went by before the machines could be returned to full operation. As a way of protecting equipment from this kind of accident, some computer centers mount large rolls of plastic sheeting on the walls near the computers, so that the plastic can be pulled out at the first drop of water.

Carbon dioxide gas effectively starves a fire of oxygen, forms no corrosive compounds and leaves no residue to clean up. Yet it is rarely used to extinguish major fires involving computer systems; in concentrations high enough to suppress a fire, it can also suffocate humans. In one alarming incident involving this gas, an automatic carbon dioxide fire-fighting system located under the raised floor of a computer installation, where most of the facility's cables were concealed, discharged accidentally one day. Computer personnel evacuated the room without incident, but the dense gas settled into the rooms on the floor below, nearly suffocating several people at work there.

A product called Halon has often been enlisted as the first line of defense in fire control for computer systems. In concentrations of less than 10 percent, this expensive, specially formulated gas effectively smothers flames yet poses no danger of asphyxiation. In a typical application, smoke and heat detectors automatically trigger the release of Halon to suppress any flames that might be present. But Halon is not a coolant, so it must be used in tandem with a sprinkler system. If enough heat is generated by the fire before the Halon puts it out, the sprinklers may go off after all, with resulting water damage.

BRACING FOR THE INEVITABLE
It is axiomatic that diligence in the pursuit of security offers no guarantees. For that reason, government agencies and companies that depend on computers find it prudent to develop and thoroughly test a so-called disaster-recovery plan (DRP). Without one, bouncing back from an emergency may be impossible. In essence, such a plan provides for quick replacement of ruined computers with functioning ones and for equally fast restoration of programs, data and the telephone communications links upon which a system depends. As illustrated by the case of a bank in Minnesota, a disaster-recovery plan can go a long way toward helping a company weather a catastrophe. On Thanksgiving Day, 1982, a fire virtually destroyed Minneapolis' Norwest Bank, causing an estimated $75 million in damage to three major divisions of the bank—pension and profit sharing, data processing and international operations. But all three divisions were back in business at other locations in just two days.

A key element in Norwest's successful recovery—and the cornerstone of all good DRPs—was a provision for storing backup copies of computer programs and data at a secure location well away from the organization's computer center. Hundreds of companies specializing in computer security rent storage for safeguarding backup tapes and disks. For maximum protection against break-ins, bombs or natural disasters, many such installations are built underground or into mountainsides. One fills a space, formerly occupied by a subway-maintenance facility, that extends 100 feet and spans two city blocks below the World Trade Center in New York City.

A typical backup facility stores its customers' computer information and software in a nondescript building where temperature and humidity are rigidly controlled. Multiple alarm systems, guards and surveillance by closed-circuit television ensure that no one can sneak into the building to steal or vandalize the materials deposited there. To protect data and software in transit, operators of some storage sites even provide 24-hour pickup and delivery service in armored, climate-controlled vans.

A few companies go a step further by establishing sites that make it possible for an organization with no fallback computers of its own to resume operations almost before the dust of a disaster has settled. These places come in two forms, known as cold sites and hot sites. A cold site is a room that has been fully outfitted with computer necessities—communications gear, air conditioning and power—but no computers. They are installed after a disaster. A hot site has backup computers and allied equipment plugged in and ready to go. Membership in a hot site can cost $6,000 a month—as much as six times the tariff for a cold site. The higher fee may seem reasonable to businesses such as banks and to government agencies that can ill afford even a day's suspension of operations.

THE HUMAN ELEMENT

A disaster-recovery plan, complete with provisions for off-premises storage and backup processing sites, may also be needed if a company is to withstand the extraordinary variety of outrages that humans have committed against computer systems. People have set them aflame with Molotov cocktails; bombed them with plastique, the terrorist's general-purpose explosive; stabbed them with screwdrivers; and short-circuited them with ordinary keys. One computer was severely beaten by a woman with the spiked heel of her shoe.

As if this arsenal were not enough, rumors and unverified reports of other anticomputer weapons often make the rounds. During the late 1960s, for example, widely circulated stories focused on the purported danger of hand-held magnets. A disgruntled employee armed with a small magnet was said to have erased data from thousands of magnetic tapes in a single night. As it turned out, experiments by the U.S. National Bureau of Standards proved that small magnets were in fact poor weapons indeed for use against electronic data. To erase magnetization of particles of iron oxide on a tape, the magnet must be held no more than a fraction of an inch away. Even then, only the outermost tape layer is affected; the reel must be unwound to get at the rest. Experts point out that simply spilling a cup of coffee on a disk or a tape is likely to be a more efficient weapon against magnetic data.

Some attacks against computers are extemporaneous, incited perhaps by momentary frustration or irritation with the victimized machines. But other assaults are planned and executed with cold-blooded precision by those who would attack society through its computers. Some incidents have caused great damage. For example, during the height of the Vietnam War, in 1970, American antiwar activists set off a bomb outside the Army Mathematics Research Center at the University of Wisconsin, killing a young graduate student working there after hours. By one estimate, the material losses—including buildings, computer hardware and a 20-year accumulation of research data—represented an investment of more than $18 million.

During the 1970s, in Europe, terrorists armed variously with submachine guns, bombs and Molotov cocktails mounted dozens of guerrilla-style assaults on computer installations. Unlike the attacks in the United States, these incidents extended beyond military or related targets to a broad array of civilian computer

A Mountain Fortress for Vital Computers

Perhaps the most thoroughly fortified computer facility in the world is the command post of the North American Aerospace Defense Command (NORAD), the binational mission charged with the air defense of the United States and Canada. More than 80 computers are buried in a subterranean city deep inside Colorado's Cheyenne Mountain. Cocooned by solid granite, the self-contained complex is built to withstand virtually any conceivable natural disaster or act of sabotage or war, barring a direct multimegaton nuclear strike.

In the early 1960s, more than 690,000 tons of rock were carved out of the mountain to create nearly three miles of interconnected tunnels and caverns. A roadway that runs east and west through the granite redoubt doubles as the central air-supply duct and is guarded around the clock. Massive, blastproof steel doors give entry from the roadway to a complex of 15 freestanding buildings occupying stone chambers that are 56 to 60 feet high. When the doors are shut, the only link to the outside is a deeply buried web of electronic communication cables.

Many of the details about the NORAD compound are secret. But on these and on the following two pages, an artist's renderings based on unclassified information illustrate some of the defenses that were developed to preserve this computer nerve center from physical harm.

Seventeen hundred feet beneath Cheyenne Mountain's rugged wilderness peak, the NORAD command post lies in a four-and-a-half-acre catacomb of granite caverns separated by huge pillars of intact rock. Four granite reservoirs and a 500,000-gallon diesel storage tank contain enough water and fuel to sustain the facility for 30 days.

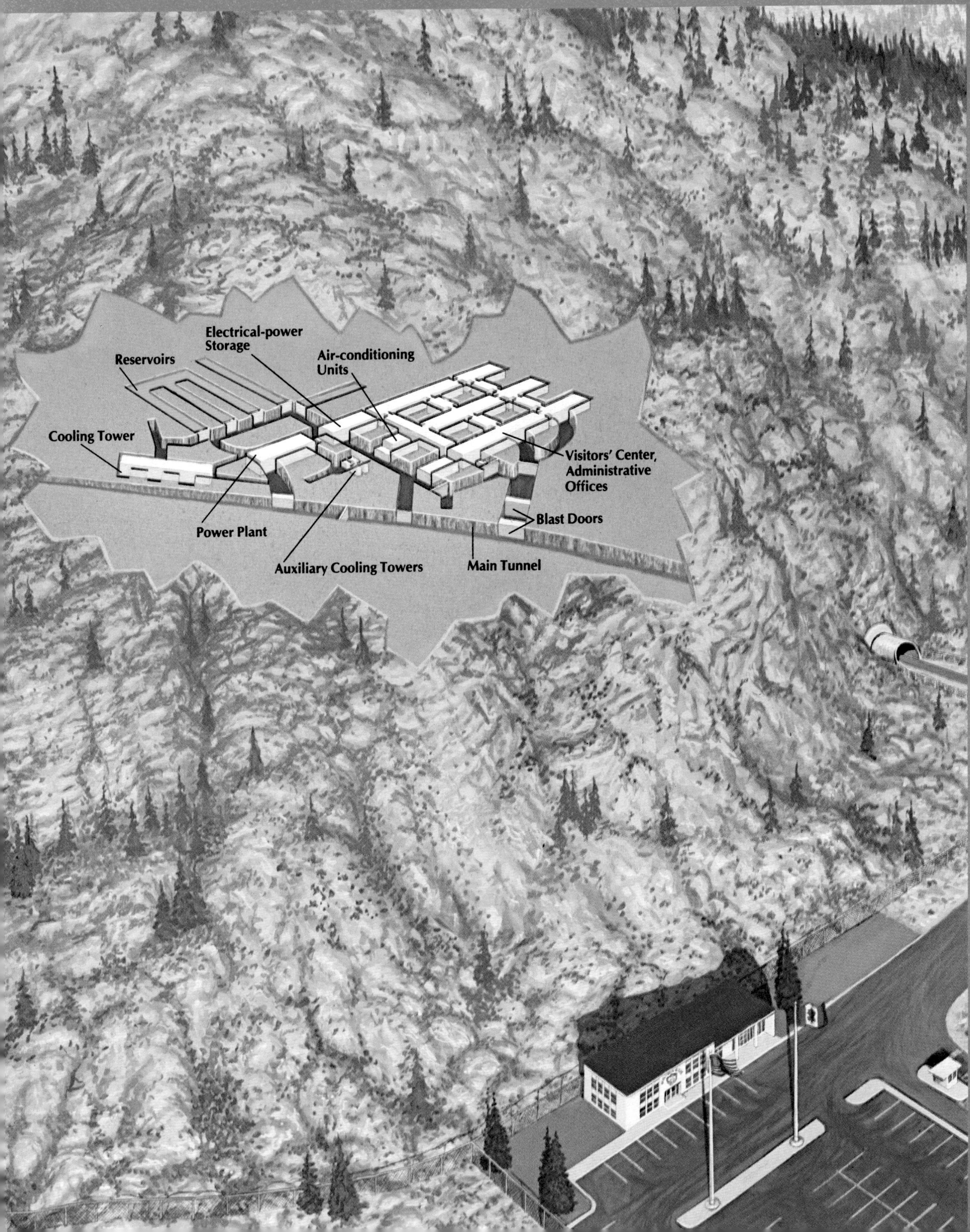

Reservoirs

Electrical-power
Storage

Air-conditioning
Units

Cooling Tower

Visitors' Center,
Administrative
Offices

Power Plant

Blast Doors

Auxiliary Cooling Towers

Main Tunnel

2

A Mountain Fortress for Vital Computers

BLASTPROOF PORTALS

To enter the NORAD complex, a visitor must travel into the mountain on the main road and turn off to pass through a pair of three-foot-thick steel doors that weigh 25 tons apiece. The outer door is designed to close flush with the rock wall of the roadway, which is open at either end. The roadway thus acts to channel heat and percussion from an explosion through the mountain and away from the doors and the complex behind them.

A SHOCKPROOF STRUCTURE

Each building in the complex rests in its own granite cavern on steel springs that let the structure roll with any shock waves that penetrate the mountain; no part of the building touches the rock. Friction dampers, like giant shock absorbers, further reduce the shaking that could result from an earthquake or a nuclear explosion. Wire mesh on the walls protects communication and power cables from rockfalls. To counter the tendency of granite to shift under its own weight, expandable bolts, ranging in length from six to 32 feet, are inserted into the rockface to form a compressed layer that strengthens the walls of the caverns.

facilities, including those of banks, government agencies, universities and especially big multinational corporations.

Even so, computer sabotage is no everyday occurrence. One study documented only 54 cases of computer sabotage worldwide between 1969 and 1981. Of those, half were confirmed as having been carried out by the Red Brigades, the most notorious of Italy's extreme left-wing terrorist organizations, and other terrorist groups. The attacks, which typically involved setting off explosives or dousing computer systems with gasoline before torching them, showed ample evidence of meticulous planning and execution. A series of 10 raids by the Red Brigades over a two-year period beginning in 1976 resulted, on average, in damages approaching a million dollars. One incident, the bombing of the Italian Motor Vehicle Ministry, destroyed so much data that nearly two years passed before the ministry had a reasonable idea of who in the country owned cars and trucks or had licenses to drive them.

CITIES AT THE MERCY OF SABOTEURS
In Japan, a well-organized gang of left-wing activists, sympathetic to railroad workers who had staged a wildcat strike, shut down the commuter-train systems of Tokyo, Osaka and five other cities in 1985. Led by members of the Middle Core Faction, a group best known for its violent anti-American demonstrations and opposition to the construction of an international airport near Narita, the vandals used wire cutters to sever some computer cables and detonated crude kerosene bombs to burn or blow up others at more than 20 locations. The attacks began at 3 a.m., but the damage passed unnoticed until two hours later. When railroad officials attempted to start the trains for the morning rush hour, they found the system hopelessly paralyzed.

The disruption deprived more than 10 million commuters of their customary mode of transportation. In Tokyo, huge traffic jams developed as those who usually took the train added their cars to already-crowded freeways leading into the city. Schools closed for lack of students and teachers. To prevent further disruption, nearly 5,000 police were dispatched to subway stations. By noon, service had been only partially restored.

Terrorist propaganda that often accompanies such sabotage focuses on the computer as a symbol. Radical ideologues perceive it as an instrument of capitalistic oppression. "Computers are the favorite instrument of the powerful," said a spokesperson for a French terrorist cell in a public statement. "They are used to classify, to control and to repress." This group, which has claimed responsibility for several attacks, asserted that its members included computer professionals "well placed to know the present and future dangers of computer systems." The organization calls itself CLODO, French slang for "tramp" and an acronym for words that translate loosely as "Committee for the Liquidation and Misappropriation of Computers."

To prevent the liquidation and misappropriation of computers, security experts recommend old-fashioned physical defenses such as locks, fences, lighting and thick, windowless masonry construction. Guards and alarms are a necessary part of the protection of even the stoutest building, since no fence is unclimbable and no lock impervious to a determined effort to break it. Even a thick concrete wall is vulnerable to the resourceful. According to a U.S. government security manual, intruders equipped with a so-called hammer-drill—an electric tool that hammers as it drills—and a sledgehammer can break a hole through a five-and-a-half-inch reinforced concrete wall in less than six minutes.

MODERN SOLUTIONS TO ANCIENT PROBLEMS

To reduce the number and expense of guards, a variety of surveillance devices is available to help watch out for intruders. In addition to closed-circuit television, for example, there are ultrasonic systems that fill a room with high-frequency sound waves, which are broadcast in a certain pattern. As the waves bounce off the walls of the room and the objects in it, the reflections form another pattern. A sensitive microphone picks up the reflected sound waves, and a control unit continually compares the pattern of the reflections with the pattern of the waves as originally broadcast. Someone entering the room disturbs the relationship between the two patterns; the system senses the change and sets off an alarm.

Electronic locks and keys can replace conventional ones to control access to particularly sensitive areas, such as a computer room or a data library. In one arrangement, the electronic key consists of a miniature radio transmitter embedded in a badge worn by the employee. As the employee approaches the door, a signal transmitted by the badge is picked up by a special radio receiver on the wall, causing the door to open automatically. This proximity-release system can also be programmed to verify that a person is authorized to enter at that specific time. Other methods of access control require verification of some human physical characteristic, such as the shape of a hand or the whorls of a fingerprint, before admission is granted (pages 45-57).

As ingenious as they are, electronic keys and physical-verification devices cannot prevent the practice known as piggybacking or tailgating. An intruder seeking to gain entry to a computer room, for example, waits near an entrance, perhaps carrying an armload of tapes or disks for camouflage. When an employee opens the door, the intruder slips into the restricted area before the door shuts.

Rather than relying on employees to challenge such behavior, some companies install a floor-to-ceiling turnstile or a device called a mantrap to bar piggybacking (page 43). A door at one end of the mantrap allows entry from the unsecured part of the facility; a door at the other end permits access.to the computer room only after the person has been identified as an authorized user.

Though virtually impossible to fool, a mantrap has limitations. For example, it can be a bottleneck for those who must pass through it and in some cases can create traffic jams that attract unwanted attention. In one instance, a bank converted an old factory building into a computer center. To disguise the building's new function from potential intruders, bank officials did not post any signs identifying the structure and made no effort to dress up the dingy exterior. For ultimate security, a mantrap was installed at the entrance. At 8 a.m. on the first day of operation, data-processing employees reporting for work formed a queue two blocks long as they waited to pass through the mantrap one at a time. Motorists creeping along in morning rush-hour traffic gawked at the line and must have wondered why such a nicely dressed crowd was apparently so eager to get into a grimy old building.

The bank's solution to this dilemma eliminated the conspicuous queue of waiting employees but undercut the mantrap's security value: Every morning, guards flung open the mantrap doors and visually checked the identity cards of the employees filing past.

Embarrassing wrinkles of this sort usually get ironed out ahead of time by a thorough rehearsing of procedures and even by the staging of simulated assaults on the security system. In England, for example, a team of consultants that includes a former Scotland Yard detective specializes in computer-center break-ins. With the aid of hired actors who assume the role of intruder, the team probes for weaknesses in a center's protective armor.

The costs of all this safety—from special consultants to fortress-like construction and high-tech access control—can run into the millions of dollars at a large computer center. But an organization may get some of its investment back. One U.S. insurance company that recognizes the value of top-flight computer security reduces premiums for security-conscious clients by as much as half.

A MATTER OF TREACHERY

For all the money that is spent on protection, one aspect of computer security remains problematical. By far the most serious threat stems not from the intruders that tight security keeps out but from the ranks of trusted employees it is designed to let in: the programmers, operators, supervisors, data-entry clerks and others who use, service and maintain the computers.

These insiders commit an alarming number of computer crimes and abuses, in an astonishing variety of ways. At one extreme, they act out of political conviction. Terrorists' arson and bomb attacks against computer facilities in Europe often could not occur without the collusion of inside sympathizers. But more commonly, people assault computers for personal reasons. Sometimes the impetus may be simple frustration. In North Carolina, a computer operator became so exasperated with the machine that he pulled out a pistol and shot it. In the heavily guarded office of the U.S. Solicitor General in Washington, D.C., an unidentified insider once urinated on a computer.

Other insiders may strike out at the machines as a way of getting back at the boss. Belden Menkus, an independent security consultant, has related the tale of a computer-tape librarian at an insurance company in Hartford, Connecticut, who was having simultaneous affairs with two men in the data-processing division. This real-life soap opera stirred so much turmoil in the computer center that she was fired. While serving out her 30 days' notice, however, she took a librarian's revenge. Methodically, she began work on the data tapes in her charge, misfiling or mislabeling many of them. The rest of the tapes she erased with a degausser, a device that generates a strong magnetic field and is used in computer facilities for wiping unwanted data from old tapes before reusing or discarding them. The librarian's handiwork, which was not discovered until the day after her departure, threw the company's records into chaos. According to Menkus, "It cost the insurance company $10 million to recreate the data this woman had destroyed."

The standard measures for preventing insiders from abusing company computer systems or profiting from them—careful screening of job applicants, counseling for employees with personal problems, restriction of physical access to those who genuinely require it—provide some answers, but not all. In order to be certain that none of their computer specialists run amuck, employers would

Setting a Mantrap against Intruders

Protecting a facility from intruders requires verifying the identity of everyone seeking entry. In 1974, Dallas-based computer manufacturer Texas Instruments began routing access to its own data-processing center through a double-doored device known as a mantrap. Under the control of a computerized sentinel, the mantrap employs three separate verification techniques. Every authorized user of the facility is identified by an individual pass number and by two physical characteristics: voice and weight.

Upon enrollment in the system, a person repeats 16 different words into a device that translates the distinctive sound waves into digital form; this is stored as a template in the computer's memory (*pages 46-47*). At the same time, to give the computer a combination of identifying characteristics that would be difficult for an impostor to fake, the user's weight is recorded. The weight identification also prevents another person from trying to sneak through, or piggyback, on the valid access of an authorized user. If the weight is more than 40 pounds over the registered weight, the computer assumes that a second person is in the booth and signals for another pass number.

① After entering the identification booth, a user punches a pass number on a 12-button key pad, signaling the computer to retrieve the voice template and weight record registered by the person assigned that number.

② Through an overhead speaker, the computer broadcasts a four-word phrase randomly selected from the 16 words previously registered.

③ The user repeats the phrase into the microphone; the sounds are digitized for comparison with the record on file.

④ If the voice patterns match and the weight on the floor scale is no more than 40 pounds over the weight on record, the exit door leading into the data-processing center will automatically unlock. If a user is not verified after seven tries, a security officer investigates.

have to probe the psychic depths of every insider, a prospect as distasteful as it would be impractical.

How hidden human quirks can erupt in bizarre behavior is illustrated in a classic case of computer abuse. It began in 1970 when the Burroughs B3500 computer operated by an insurance company in Denver started acting up. Time after time, the internal disk drive shorted out, causing a head crash. Company officials assumed the computer was to blame, and Burroughs dispatched its expert fixers. They replaced the internal drive several times and even installed a backup drive, all to no avail. The experts then hypothesized that fluctuations in power might be the cause, so they installed new wiring, motor generators and circuit breakers. Nothing worked. Over a period of two years, the disk drive crashed at least 56 times, shutting down the computer for an average of eight hours on each occasion.

Costs to Burroughs and losses by the company had mounted to $500,000 before someone suggested sabotage as the cause. Since the short circuits always occurred at night, suspicion naturally fell on the operator who ran the computer during that shift. A veteran employee with a clean record, he seemed unlikely as a candidate for saboteur. Besides, he always appeared concerned and helpful to the mystified engineers whom his emergency telephone calls summoned from their sleep in the middle of the night.

Nevertheless, the security staff concealed a closed-circuit television camera and recorder above the ceiling in the computer room. On the second night of surveillance, their efforts were rewarded. As the camera watched, the man pulled a key from the pocket of his jeans, opened a cabinet door and, in a burst of sparks, stuck the key into the innards of the disk drive.

Confronted with the videotaped evidence the following day, the man confessed. His mischief began, he said, after he had become lonely at work one night. He wanted so desperately to go home that he was filled with an overpowering desire to shut down the machine that kept him there all night. Sabotaging the computer satisfied that urge and brought him something more. Every time he got the night-shift blues, he simply stuck his key into the disk drive, summoned the engineers and, as if by magic, found that he not only was no longer alone but was the center of attention and excitement.

Tests of Identity

Restricting access to a computer system requires a sure means of identifying authorized users. Generally, identity can be established by something a person knows, such as a password; by something a person has, such as a key; and by something a person is or does—some intrinsic physical trait. In practice, passwords are often forgotten by their owners and are subject to discovery by others; keys may be copied, lost or stolen. But the third option is nearly immune to such mishaps.

Every human being is distinguished by many unique physical characteristics. Thousands of people may have the same height, weight, or hair color, for example; but no two individuals sign their names identically, nor do they have precisely the same designs on their fingertips. Both signatures and fingerprints have been used for identification since long before the age of computers. However, as explained on the following pages, they are now being examined in unexpected ways by so-called biometric devices, instruments that perform mathematical analyses of biological characteristics. Moreover, other unique physical traits—including footprints, lipprints, the pattern of blood vessels in the retina and the vibrations of the voice—are subject to similar examination.

Those responsible for maintaining the security of computer centers—or, for that matter, of bank vaults, military installations and other sensitive areas—must consider several factors in choosing a biometric security system. Ideally, the error rate—that is, the mistaken acceptance of outsiders and the rejection of authorized insiders—should be extremely low. This means the system must be able to spot counterfeits while making allowances for normal variations—for example, in the voice of a person suffering from a cold. The time required to enroll people in the system—that is, to make a computerized record of their physical traits—should not be excessive; similarly, verification of a user's identity should take as little time as possible. Thus, the system cannot impose undue inconvenience, such as requiring people to remove their shoes and socks for footprint verification. Finally, the expense of the system must be commensurate with the value of the material being protected.

Turning Data into a Personal Template

Most biometric identification systems, whether they analyze a person's fingerprints, voice or signature, have certain features in common. For one thing, they usually require data from the real world—light or sound, for instance—to be converted into an information stream a computer can understand. As illustrated below, the computer receives a continuous flow of data from its sensors, in the form of an electrical signal that increases and decreases in voltage. In a system that uses fingerprints for identification, for example, the sensor will read the print's ridges as alternating areas of light and dark and will represent them as rising and falling voltage intensities.

The continuous electrical flow is called an analog signal; its

Providing data. In the first step, the user submits samples of the trait to be measured to a specialized sensor. For some systems the enrollee might provide speech or signature samples; in others the computer might record fingerprint, hand, or retina features.

Creating an analog signal. The data is converted to an electrical signal, with high and low voltages representing such traits as strong and weak acoustic power in a voice, heavy and light pressure in a signature, or bright and dark regions in an image.

Sampling. To convert the fluctuating but continuous analog signal into the computer's digital code, the computer samples the signal, isolating and measuring individual moments of the continuous flow.

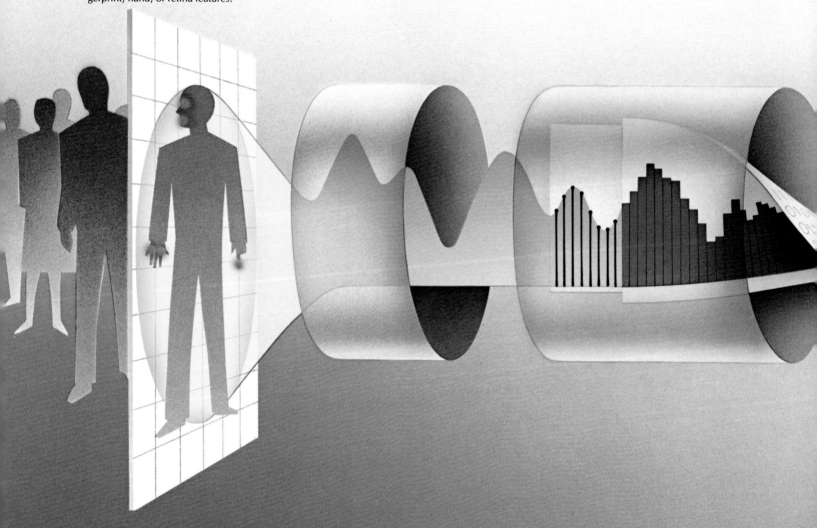

voltage changes serve as an analogy for nonelectrical changes in the real world. An analog-to-digital converter measures the voltage of the analog input hundreds of times a second, thereby dividing the continuous signal into a series of discrete signals called samples. Each sample is equivalent to one frame in a movie: By itself it represents only one frozen moment of input, but in sequence with other samples it makes a recognizable facsimile of the original continuous signal. The computer then assigns a numerical value to each sample and stores those numbers as binary digits, or bits.

In practice, minor variations occur from one time to the next when a person is inspected by a biometric security sys-

tem. No signature is duplicated exactly each time it is signed; the voice can change with age, sickness and stress; and a fingerprint's impression may be smeared, placed off-center or partially obscured. Thus, at the time a new user is enrolled, most systems follow a procedure that will allow for some variations in the future. Instead of making only one initial reading, the system takes several. These are then manipulated according to a formula to create an electronic template of the identifying characteristic. Then, when the user's identity must be verified later, the computer is given a prescribed amount of leeway before having to reject a sample for not being a close enough match.

Digitizing the signal. The computer assigns each sample a numerical value within a prescribed range and translates the values into the form of the binary digits one and zero; the computer reads the bits as a sequence of on-off electronic pulses.

Processing. The digitized signal is processed by an algorithm, a set of instructions in the system's software that manipulates the binary digits, often condensing them for the most efficient storage.

Making the template. Usually, to allow for minor variations, several readings of an identifying trait are taken and then merged mathematically. The result is an electronic ID the system can refer to every time the enrolled user seeks access.

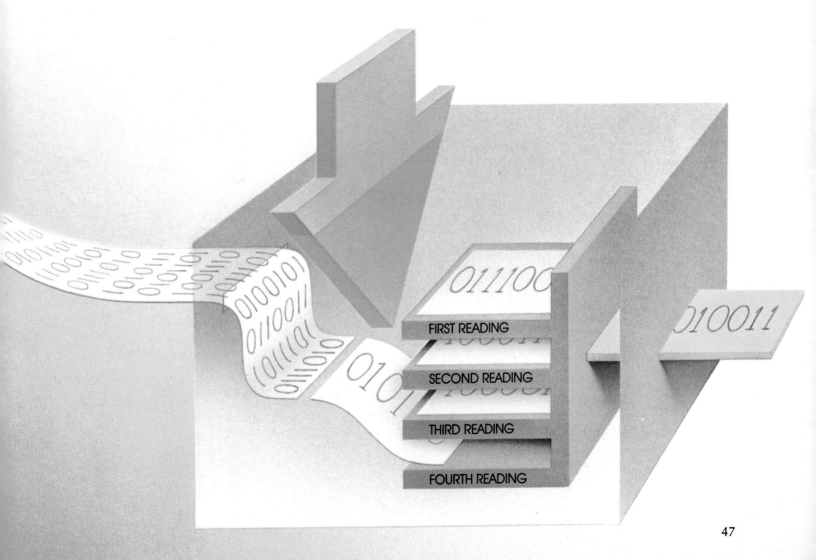

FIRST READING

SECOND READING

THIRD READING

FOURTH READING

Measuring the Act of Writing

A user at a remote terminal signs for access to a multi-user computer system. A signature template stored in the central computer verifies the signer's identity.

Sensors for Three Signals

This biometric pen converts a signature into a set of three electrical signals by means of piezoelectric transducers, ceramic devices that generate measurable voltages in response to stress. One transducer senses changes in the writer's downward pressure on the penpoint; farther up the pen shaft, two transducers set at right angles to each other measure vertical and horizontal movement. Although the computer does not need a visible signature, the pen also includes an ink cartridge; tests have shown that people sign more naturally if they see what they are writing.

Pressure Sensor

Acceleration Sensors

Thomas Worthington

When human observers verify a signature, they normally concentrate on the way the name looks. A biometric verification system takes a different measure, judging a signature not by its appearance but by the dynamics of the signing process—the changes in force as the writer's hand touches down lightly for one stroke, harder on the next.

The system's sensors may be incorporated into a sensitive pad on which the signature is written, or they may be built into the signing pen. The verification pen illustrated here was developed by a team of IBM scientists directed by Thomas Worthington, whose signature is used in this explanation. Typically, the pen is attached by a flexible cable to a terminal that is part of a multi-user system.

Signals from the pen's sensors are translated into a trio of electrical wave forms, one representing changes in downward pressure, the other two representing acceleration along the pen's vertical and horizontal axes. The crossing of a *t*, for example, would register as a high point in the horizontal and a low point in the vertical wave form, whereas the dotting of an *i* would produce a peak in the pressure-change wave while leaving both of the acceleration wave forms relatively flat. A curved or diagonal stroke, for its part, would generate action in both acceleration signals.

To become enrolled in the signature verification system, a person typically writes six signatures, from which the computer chooses two samples to make a verification template. Later, when the enrollee seeks access to the system, the computer will request the person's identification number, retrieve the appropriate verification template from memory, then ask for a signature. Only if the dynamics of the signature match those of the template closely enough will the computer allow the person access to the system.

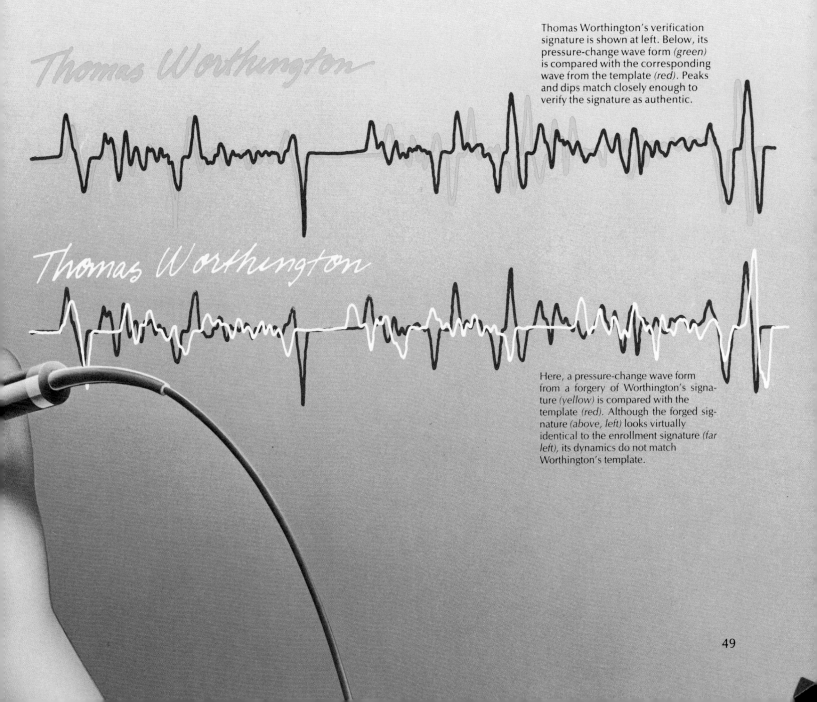

Thomas Worthington's verification signature is shown at left. Below, its pressure-change wave form (green) is compared with the corresponding wave from the template (red). Peaks and dips match closely enough to verify the signature as authentic.

Here, a pressure-change wave form from a forgery of Worthington's signature (yellow) is compared with the template (red). Although the forged signature (above, left) looks virtually identical to the enrollment signature (far left), its dynamics do not match Worthington's template.

The Individuality
of a Vocal Signature

Progress in voice biometrics could lead to the development of a system that identifies authorized users over the telephone and gives them access via remote terminals.

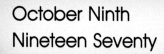

October Ninth
Nineteen Seventy

The waveform below indicates the fluctuating signal generated by the spoken phrase (a date memorable to the user). The spectrogram *(bottom)* pinpoints unique formants by graphing component frequencies.

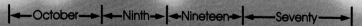

|←—October—→|←—Ninth—→|←—Nineteen—→|←—Seventy—→|

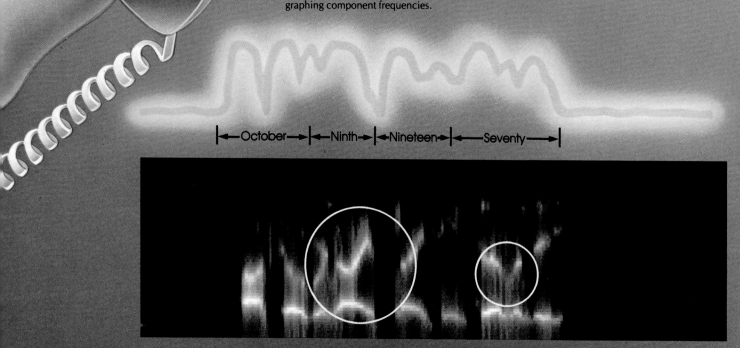

Largely still in the experimental stage, reliable computer systems for voice verification would be useful for both on-site and remote user identification. The voice verifier described here is a developmental system at American Telephone and Telegraph. Enrollment would require the user to repeat a particular phrase several times. The computer would sample, digitize and store each reading of the phrase and then, from the data, build a voice signature that would make allowances for an individual's characteristic variations.

For purposes of analysis, the computer first focuses mainly on the simplest characteristic of a voice: its acoustic strength. This fluctuates during a spoken phrase from silence to varying degrees of loudness. To isolate personal characteristics within these fluctuations, the computer breaks the sound into its component frequencies and analyzes how they are distributed. On a spectrogram—a visual representation of the voice *(bottom)*—the high-amplitude frequencies are indicated by bright spots called formants. The precise appearance of the formants is determined by the unique shape and movement of a speaker's lips, tongue, throat and vocal cords.

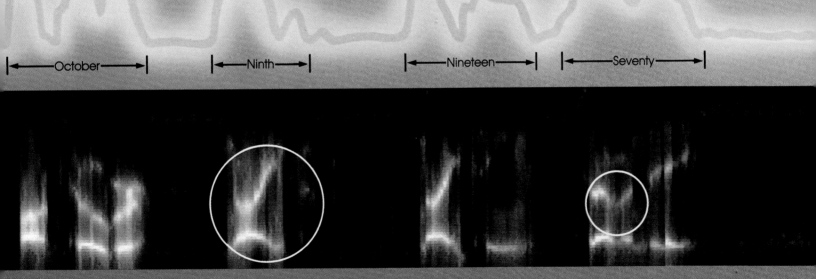

Oc-to-ber . . . Nin-th . . . Nine-teen . . . Se-ven-ty . . .

Even when the speaker deliberately draws out the phrase, the characteristic formants of the voice signature remain constant electronic diagrams of the unique configurations of the speaker's mouth and vocal cords.

|←——October——→| |←—Ninth—→| |←——Nineteen——→| |←—Seventy—→|

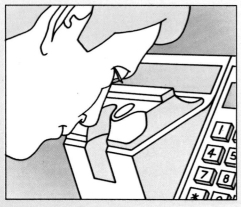

Patterns in the Eye

To enroll in the system or to verify identity, the user looks into an eyepiece, focuses on a designated point behind the lens and receives a low-intensity infrared scan.

An infrared sensor in the scanning device perceives blood vessels as a dark pattern against lighter retinal tissue. A microprocessor in the unit digitizes this image by assigning a numerical value—from zero for the darkest gray to 4,095 for the lightest—to each of 320 sampled points.

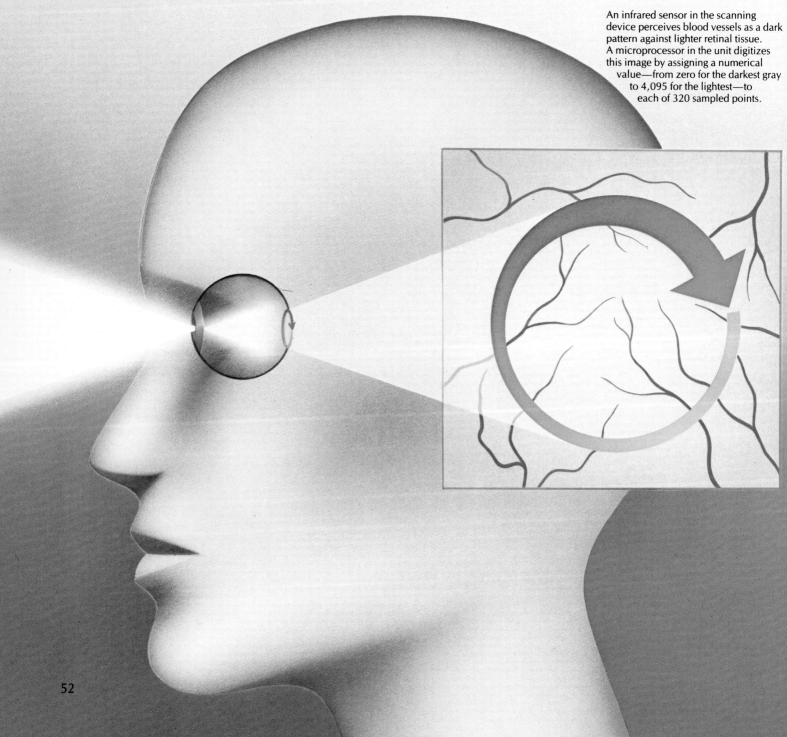

Every person carries at the back of each eyeball a pattern as distinct and inimitable as a fingerprint. But unlike a fingerprint, the fine tracery of blood vessels in the retinal tissue is an invisible identifier that cannot be recorded manually. It cannot even be photographed with an ordinary camera.

The biometric identification system illustrated on these pages uses an infrared beam, which scans the retina in a circular path. A detector in the eyepiece of the device measures the intensity of the light as it is reflected from different points. Because blood vessels do not absorb and reflect the same quantities of infrared as the surrounding tissue, the eyepiece sensor records the vessels as an intricate dark pattern against a lighter background. The device samples light inten-

sity at 320 points around the path of the scan, producing a digital profile of the vessel pattern. (Only one inspection is necessary, since a person's retinaprint, or retinal signature, does not change as the voice or a written signature does.) The algorithm in the system's software then compresses the digital profile into a reference template.

Enrollment can take as little as 30 seconds and verification can be even faster: The user types in an identification number to call up the reference template from the computer's memory and then looks into the eyepiece for a retinal scan. In only a second and a half, the computer compares the scan results with the template and grants access if the two signatures are a close enough match.

The retina-pattern template from the eye at left and opposite can be drawn as a waveform (above), with peaks for the brightest areas of the image and valleys for the darkest. The computer creates the template by manipulating the digitized scan data according to a formula and storing the result in memory as a sequence of binary digits.

The image at left represents another—and markedly different—retinal pattern, and its waveform signature reflects that difference. Manufacturers of this system assert that when the system is set to accurate specifications it will let an unauthorized user through only one time in a million.

Recording the Geometry of the Hand

Schoolchildren who trace their hands in art class quickly discover that no two are exactly alike. Shown here is a biometric security system that uses this principle to verify an individual's identity. Instead of a sketch, the system employs a sophisticated scanning device to record the unique measurements of each person's hand.

A user enrolls in a so-called hand geometry system by placing one hand on the metal plate of a reading device, positioning the middle and ring fingers on either side of a small peg and aligning all the fingers along narrow grooves slotted with glass (right). An overhead light shines down on the hand, and a sensor underneath the plate scans the fingers through the glass slots, recording light intensity from the fingertips to the webbing where the fingers join the palm. The device measures each finger to within $\frac{1}{10,000}$ of an inch, marking where the finger begins and ends by the varying intensities of light. The information is digitized and stored in the system as a template or coded on a magnetic-strip ID card.

Despite the uniqueness of individual hands, hand geometry identification is not foolproof. For example, if a user with long fingernails enrolled in the system wearing heavy nail polish, the sensor could not detect the true ends of the fingertips, which would be hidden by the dark nails. The computer would thus be unable to verify the person's identity if she tried to gain access after removing the nail polish.

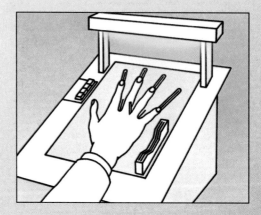

With light shining from above, a sensor beneath the metal plate scans the user's hand, taking measurements of the light intensity of each finger from tip to palm.

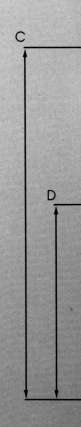

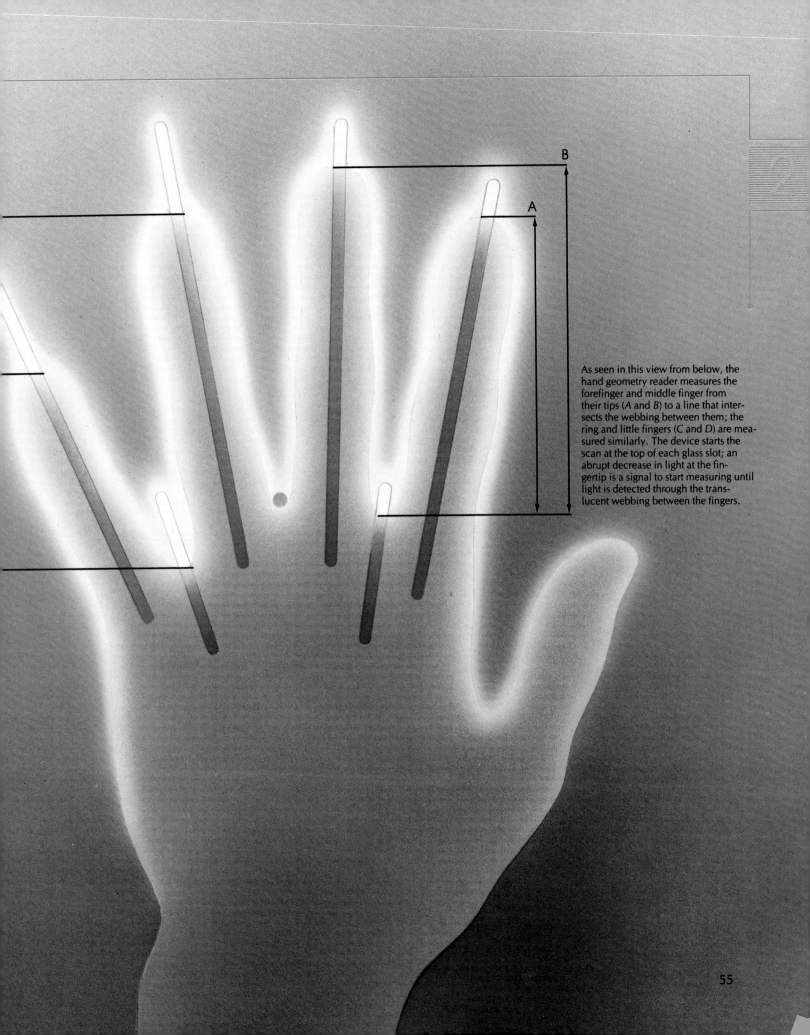

As seen in this view from below, the hand geometry reader measures the forefinger and middle finger from their tips (A and B) to a line that intersects the webbing between them; the ring and little fingers (C and D) are measured similarly. The device starts the scan at the top of each glass slot; an abrupt decrease in light at the fingertip is a signal to start measuring until light is detected through the translucent webbing between the fingers.

Mapping the Intricacies of a Fingerprint

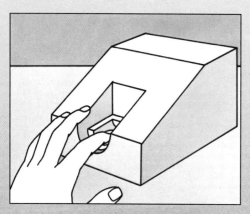

In a fingerprint verification system, the user places one finger on a glass plate; light flashes inside the machine, reflects off the fingerprint and is picked up by an optical scanner. The scanner transmits the information to the computer for analysis.

At the core of the print, data from each pixel (its numerical gray-scale value) is fed into an algorithm that analyzes clusters of pixels to determine where ridge splits and endings occur *(marked here by red patches).*

The system is designed to focus on one square inch *(below)*, centered on the core of the print *(shown enlarged at right)*. The computer samples data from this area on a grid of 500 by 500 picture elements, or pixels.

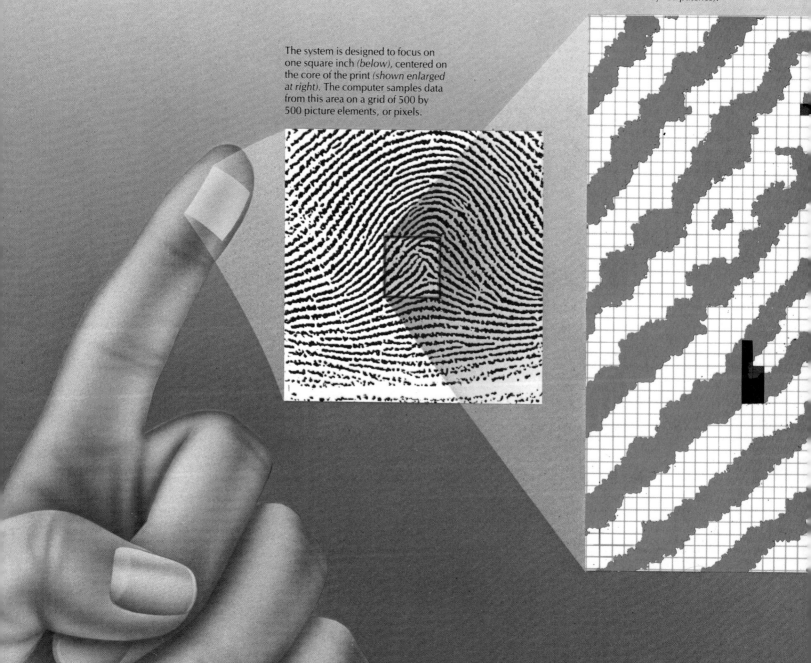

Fingerprint identification is based on the anatomical truth that no two fingerprints are exactly alike; each has a unique pattern of prominent features such as arches, loops and whorls. But trying to identify an individual print from these characteristics alone is often problematic. If a print's impression is smudged or distorted by dirt, for instance, the patterns may be sufficiently incomplete to make a positive identification impossible. With the advent of computerized fingerprint systems, security experts can now verify identity by looking at so-called minutiae, smaller details and variations within the larger features.

At enrollment, data samples from a scan of the user's fingerprint are interpreted as varying degrees of gray and assigned a numerical value. This gray-scale representation is processed by a complex algorithm, which pays special attention to the places where clusters of light and dark points indicate that a ridge has divided or ended. The system is designed to analyze these minute ridge splits and endings, ascertaining their positions relative to the core of the print and to one another; the system also analyzes the angle of the ridges. These relationships remain unaltered even when a print's impression is faint, dirty or distorted.

Several readings are taken and manipulated by the algorithm to create a stored template. A user wishing to gain access to a secure area merely enters an identification number to call up the template, places the same finger in the scanner and waits a few seconds for a verification analysis. If the prints are a close enough match, access is granted.

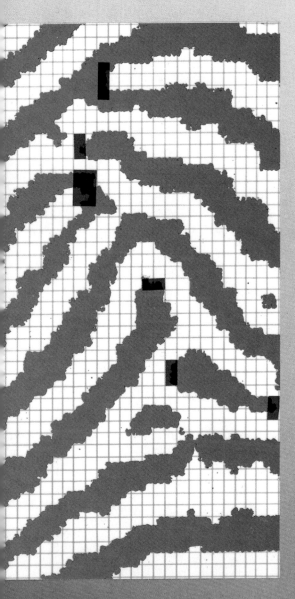

The system can read even a fingerprint that is partially illegible because of dirt, injury or insufficient pressure on the scanner. The faint print at right is from the same finger as the one at far left; the machine can recognize it by the relative positions of its minutiae.

Frequently the system has to read prints that are askew. Here, the print scanned for verification is not aligned as it was at enrollment. Despite the altered orientation of the lines, however, the distinctive placement of the minutiae remains unchanged.

Trojan Horses and Logic Bombs

Richard Streeter, a CBS Inc. executive and computer hobbyist in Fanwood, New Jersey, retired to his recreation room one summer day in 1985 to pursue a favorite diversion: checking electronic bulletin boards for new computer programs free for the taking. On this day, he used the modem attached to his computer to dial a bulletin board operated by an acquaintance on Long Island.

Streeter availed himself of a bulletin-board feature that displayed on his monitor only programs posted since he had last logged on. One offering caught his eye. As Streeter recalled several months later, the program, EGABTR, "promised to improve by 50 percent" the performance of a computer-graphics circuit board he had recently purchased. Intrigued by this claim, Streeter copied the program onto his own computer's hard disk drive, a device capable of holding 30 million bytes of information.

Reflecting on what happened next, Streeter felt that he might have been more alert to trouble. EGABTR came without instructions, an ominous sign. And the improvements it promised seemed—in retrospect, at least—too good to be true. At the time, however, Streeter eagerly tried out the new program, only to be greeted by an insolent message on the monitor: "Arf, arf! Got you!" Streeter found out what "Got you!" meant when he tried to retrieve information from his hard disk. Nothing was there. EGABTR had effectively destroyed more than 900 computer programs and documents by scrambling the computer's index to the files. Without the index, the information might as well never have existed.

EGABTR is an example of what computer-security specialists refer to as a Trojan horse. Much as warriors of ancient Greece hid inside a wooden horse presented to the city of Troy as a peace offering, a small computer program is concealed among the thousands—or even millions—of lines of instructions that constitute an otherwise legitimate piece of software. Then, when the software is running on the computer, the secret instructions lurking inside spring into action. Like the Greek soldiers who spilled out of the horse and opened the gates of Troy to the army laying siege to the city, the computer-age Trojan horse begins performing unexpected functions.

The Trojan horse—like related techniques known as logic bombs, worms and viruses—is an all-purpose tool for attacking the computer. It enables people to recruit the computer itself as an accomplice in crimes ranging from fraud to outright sabotage. Such offenses, which involve the electronic manipulation of data or programs, typically are staged so stealthily that they may go undetected for months or years. "Computer crime is a low-visibility proposition," a U.S. Department of Justice official told a Senate committee in a report submitted in 1976. "There are no smoking pistols—no blood-stained victims; often the crime is detected by sheer accident."

Since that warning, computerized attacks on computers have grown more frequent, and the attacks themselves have become more sophisticated. In addition, the potential for wrongdoing swells as more and more people gain access

In the hands of dishonest computer operators and programmers, a computer system can undergo a disturbing metamorphosis. One moment it is an obedient servant; the next it contains a hidden serpent that can steal data, ruin programs and even bring the system crashing to a halt.

to computer systems through the proliferation of both time-sharing arrangements—in which multiple users share a single large computer—and networks of computers linked by telephone.

Indeed, to security specialists charged with safeguarding data-processing systems, it must often seem that a potential intruder lurks around every corner. But the very instrument criminals seek to exploit is also the main weapon against intrusion. Using the computer as a kind of security guard, protectors of the system must find ways not only to outwit and bar entry to hackers and other knowledgeable outsiders, but also to police the clerks, programmers and other employees who have legitimate access. These trusted insiders—typically well-educated, white-collar professionals with no previous brushes with the law—pose the greatest threat. Best estimates indicate that the much-publicized young hackers and other outsiders commit only a small percentage of the computer crimes in the United States; the vast majority of such deeds are the work of insiders.

DIFFICULT CRIMES, SIMPLE CRIMES

The techniques available to computer criminals, whether insiders or outsiders, form a hierarchy of difficulty. Building a covert program such as a Trojan horse tops this pyramid, requiring programming skill as well as the guile of a con artist. Not only must a Trojan horse program be flawlessly written if it is to accomplish its author's purpose, it must also be made to appear so innocuous that an operator or a hobbyist like Streeter will allow it into the computer system under attack. Few computer workers who are criminally inclined also possess the expertise for such an assault. On the other hand, legions of individuals can lay claim to the modest skills needed to damage computer systems or steal from them by means of the comparatively simple techniques at the base of the pyramid. These methods take advantage of computers in much the same way that spies and embezzlers have for centuries exploited security weaknesses in manual record-keeping systems.

In the wake of new criminal opportunities, a new lexicon of crime has arisen. Stealing, for example, has become data disclosure. The data at issue is typically information such as trade secrets or proprietary software that thieves can sell or use to their own advantage. Three computer operators at the Encyclopaedia Britannica once copied the names and addresses of two million customers from tapes and sold them to a company specializing in direct mailing. Britannica reckoned that if the copies had not been recovered, its corporate losses would have exceeded three million dollars. In another case, a key employee of an American software company resigned in a dispute over salary and began to market his own line of similar computer programs. To develop a list of customers, he used his own computer and a modem to dial his former employer's computer. He next typed a current employee's name and guessed the right password, thus gaining admittance to the system. Then he rifled the electronic files.

A third instance of data leakage resulted in a gusher of sensitive information from a high-tech manufacturing firm in the United States. For several years, people in cities across the nation dialed into the company's 97-computer network and, unnoticed, copied vital information from data bases containing details of research and development plans, marketing strategy and financial health. In research and development alone, nearly 45 million bytes of data, roughly equal to nine copies of *Roget's International Thesaurus*, were stolen every month. In all,

data estimated to have been worth as much as several hundred million dollars was siphoned from the company's computers. A direct result of this industrial espionage was that one of the firm's competitors duplicated a proprietary electronic device and undercut its inventors by 40 percent.

Data thieves sometimes know precisely what they are looking for and ask for it by name. When they are less certain, they engage in the practice known as scavenging or browsing. They randomly search the computer's files for valuable information, sometimes finding it in the residue of data left in the computer's memory or on magnetic tapes and disks that have been incompletely erased. One customer of a time-sharing service was caught reading residual data on a temporary-storage tape. The information, left there by an oil company that also used the service, dealt with seismic exploration for new wells; the sneak had been selling it to the oil company's competitors for a nice profit.

In these cases, the greed is blatant but the actual crime debatable; reading residual data on a storage tape may or may not be against the law. Equally debatable are transgressions committed in that murky realm known as theft of computer time. Since the early days of computing, programmers have filled the machine's idle hours with their own pursuits. Indeed, electronic games grew out of the inventive use of a computer not otherwise occupied. From this innocent start, it was a short step to utilizing an employer's computer for financial gain. Employees have been caught using the company data-processing system to run football pools, to keep track of investments and, in the instance of one enterprising horse-race fan, to store a personal handicapping system.

Such transgressors are seldom prosecuted. Supervisors are aware that employees often use other office equipment, such as typewriters, for personal correspondence or to handle a moonlighting project. But time on big computers is far more valuable than time on a typewriter, and moonlighting sometimes reaches such a scale that the boss may be forced to press charges. A rare criminal case along these lines grew out of the remarkable business enterprise of two programmers at Sperry-Univac in Philadelphia. The pair spent three years—and an estimated $144,000 worth of time on the company's big Univac 90/70—operating a lucrative music-arranging sideline. They wrote a program to produce and revise

complicated orchestral arrangements and then printed out the scores, which they marketed to music stores and bands.

Perhaps because conviction for theft of computer time carried a maximum jail sentence of just one year, federal prosecutors charged the men with the more serious crimes of mail fraud and conspiracy, which carry maximum penalties of 30 years and a $15,000 fine. They were convicted, but the judge—mindful perhaps of the novelty of the case—gave them suspended sentences.

REVISING HISTORY, A BYTE AT A TIME

A more common type of computer crime is data diddling. Whether the result of a Trojan horse program slipped into a system or of a less sophisticated assault, data diddling is the unauthorized alteration of information as it goes into a computer system or the modification of data already stored there. Often petty or greedy impulses motivate people to alter computer data illicitly. A Texas college student, seated at a personal computer in his dormitory room, called up the record of his unexceptional chemistry grades, stored on a disk in the university's main computer, and gave himself better ones. An Ohio police chief called up the file of traffic offenses on a computer terminal and deleted from his own record an embarrassing reckless-driving charge.

Data diddling has also been an outlet for pent-up rage. A particularly malicious episode occurred in Salt Lake City, where a philanthropic group called the Community Action Program used a computerized telephone message to disseminate food-distribution information to the poor and elderly. Someone penetrated the system and substituted insults for assistance. Callers heard themselves excoriated as "bums," accused of "leeching on the taxpayers," and exhorted to "stop sleeping on park benches" and to "go out and get a job."

But the root of most data diddling is money—and lots of it—in the form of credit and goods, as well as cash. During the 1970s, a million-dollar data-diddling scheme in doctored credit ratings flourished in the United States. For a fee, employees at a California-based reporting agency—a private company that collects credit information about individuals for

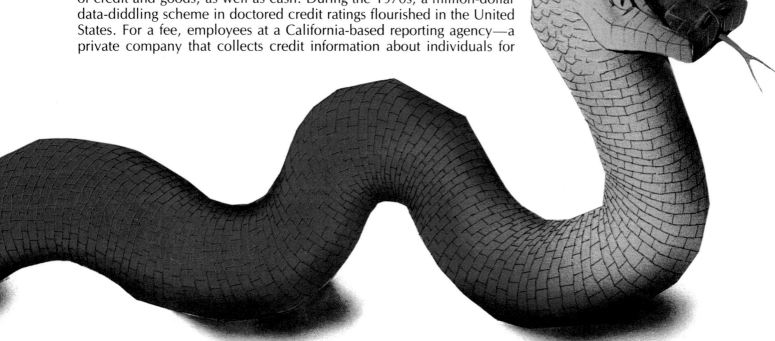

subscribers such as banks and other businesses—offered to improve anyone's credit rating by expunging questionable aspects of credit history. At other credit bureaus, workers set up satisfactory ratings for fictitious persons and then used these false ratings and identities to obtain credit cards and bank loans.

In computerized inventory-control systems, goods and their locations are commonly denoted by codes. A number changed here, a letter altered there, and quantities of goods or equipment can be diverted to an unauthorized destination, from which they then disappear. Once, this data-diddling ruse resulted in the rerouting and theft of no fewer than 217 boxcars from the now bankrupt Penn Central Railroad; in another case, South Korean technicians sidetracked for resale as much as $18 million a year in U.S. military supplies sent to their nation.

In 1971, a young college student named Jerry Schneider purloined supply-center codes from Pacific Telephone and Telegraph Company and used them to steal communications gear valued at nearly a million dollars. Arrested and convicted, Schneider repaid PT&T a mere $8,500 and served 40 days in jail. Then, at the age of 23, he became a security consultant, safeguarding computer systems against the likes of Jerry Schneider.

INSTANT RICHES FROM THE BANKING SYSTEM

During the decade after Schneider's caper, new data-diddling opportunities arose as banks and other financial institutions began to debit and credit accounts by computer. These electronic funds transfers (EFTs) became targets for computer crime. With just a few minutes at the keyboard, a clever thief can use a computer to manipulate huge sums of money over long-distance telephone wires.

A nimble con artist once staged just such a crime with the unwitting collusion of his girlfriend, a data-processing clerk at a West Coast bank. First, the man opened an account at a New York bank. Then he persuaded his girlfriend to type into the computer an order transmitting two million dollars from her employer to the New York account, explaining it as a practical joke on a computer-operator friend at the New York end of the line; the friend would understand the message as a fake, the con man said, and enjoy the charade. But as soon as the deposit was credited to the New York account, the swindler collected the two million dollars and disappeared.

Had the thief allied himself with a computer programmer, his take might have been even greater, and at less risk of discovery. Expert programmers can often contrive a more inconspicuous entry into a computer system: They can search for an opening known as a trap door. A typical trap door is a set of special instructions written into a computer's operating system—or some other program—that allows a systems manager to bypass normal security procedures to test the software before the system becomes operational. These special codes are usually erased and the trap doors closed before the computer is put to use, but sometimes they are overlooked or purposely left behind to ease maintenance, including upgrading or troubleshooting. In that event, the trap door invites abuse, enabling an intruder to enter sensitive files.

The idea that this kind of loophole can exist even in supposedly secure systems was given wide currency in the popular movie *WarGames*. In that film, the designer of a vital Department of Defense computer program creates a trap door that springs open in response to the password "Joshua." After the designer mysteriously disappears, a young hacker discovers the Joshua trap door, opens it and inadvertently sets in motion a simulated war game that threatens to culminate in actual global nuclear warfare.

In real life, computer criminals have taken advantage of existing trap doors for profit. A group of automotive engineers in Detroit once discovered such an opening after dialing into a Florida time-sharing service. Through the trap door they found the password of the service's president and thus gained entry into important proprietary software, which they proceeded to copy and use free of charge. When trap doors do not already exist, hackers have created them just for fun. Having broken into a computer system via modem, a hacker leaves behind a set of special instructions that provides future access.

MAKING MISCHIEF FROM WITHIN

In either case, once the walls have been breached, the versatile Trojan horse is an ideal tool for automating crimes such as embezzlement. To avoid arousing suspicions, embezzlers sometimes use a Trojan horse technique that security experts call the salami method—slicing ill-gotten gains into increments thin enough to go unnoticed. A bank's computer programmer, for example, could conceivably enjoy a handsome extra income by instructing the computer to subtract automatically and randomly, under the guise of service charges, 10 or 15 cents a month from many of the checking accounts it processes and then divert the funds into a dummy account. Or a programmer might profit from the fractions of pennies that result from interest calculations on savings-account deposits. Instead of having the computer distribute these individually insignificant amounts equitably among all accounts, the programmer might channel them to a single account listed under a false name. Customers would be unlikely to complain; none would lose more than pennies at a time. And auditors might never discover the embezzlement because, overall, the bank's books would balance.

Trojan horses do not all operate so subtly. Some of them, like the EGABTR program that destroyed computer hobbyist Richard Streeter's data, go off with a bang. Indeed, they are known among security specialists as logic bombs. EGABTR had a short fuse, exploding the first time it was used. More often, logic bombs are set to detonate under a particular set of conditions or, like a time bomb, at a specified moment in the future. The extent of the damage depends on the instructions. A logic bomb exploding in the Los Angeles department of water and power simply froze all of the computer's internal files, preventing anyone from using them. A French programmer, after being cashiered, left a farewell salute in the record-keeping software he had been working on. The bomb exploded two years later on New Year's Day, wiping out all the records stored on tape. Other programmers have altered software instructions to delete all names on a company's payroll if their own disappeared from the list.

On rare occasions, when a logic bomb is discovered before it detonates, it can point directly to the culprit, as an American graduate student once discovered. Operating from his own terminal on his university's time-sharing system, the student created an ingenious trap door that enabled him to command all the resources of the system and permitted him access to even the most privileged information, including the salary of the institution's president. Not one to hide

Tactics to Counter Software Pirates

Software piracy, the unauthorized copying of programs sold commercially on floppy disks, is so prevalent that analysts estimate there is one pirated program for every piece of business software sold legitimately. In some parts of the world, that ratio reaches nine to one. The annual cost to the software industry is hundreds of millions of dollars.

To stem its losses, the industry made a number of efforts during the 1980s to render copies of programs unusable. Each method involved placing a unique feature on the original program disk that could not be transferred to another disk by conventional copying methods. If the feature was missing, the program would not run.

As shown here and on the next two pages, however, pirates managed to crack each copy-protection scheme. Programs that were hard to duplicate were also unpopular with legitimate buyers who wished to copy programs onto hard disks or to make backups.

Today most software vendors have abandoned such direct tactics. They now rely more on the court to defend their goods from the software thieves.

64

his accomplishments indefinitely, he rigged a logic bomb to go off on a date long after he would have received his Ph.D. and left the university. The plan called for normal activity in the school's time-sharing system to be interrupted while all of its printers churned out a full description of his brilliant trap door and identified its architect. Then the entire system would cease to function.

But before any of this could transpire, a programmer working for the university to track down a bug, or malfunction, in the system's software stumbled upon the aberrant code of the trap door. Suspicion immediately fell on the graduate student because he was considered the most proficient computerist on campus. When officials investigated his computer data files, they found the descriptive message he had composed. With what amounted to a full confession in the hands of school officials, the logic bomb exploded in the saboteur's face.

In the commercial arena, a few vendors of custom software have borrowed from the techniques of electronic vandals, in an effort to get their money even if their work fails to fulfill its promise. This was evidently the case in an unusual tale that began to unfold in January 1982 at the Montgomery County library

Disk anatomy. Before a disk can be used, it must be formatted—divided into concentric tracks and wedgelike sectors. A disk directory keeps tabs on the sector and track coordinates of the pieces of a file, which may be scattered all over the disk.

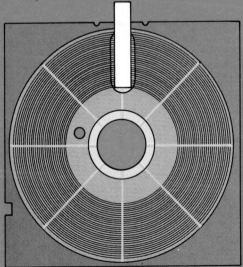

A so-called index hole through the disk's jacket and the disk itself enables the disk drive's read-write head *(white)* to orient itself by finding the first sector and track. The head makes contact with selected portions of the disk through the slot opening in the jacket.

Directory shift. If the disk directory *(red in outer tracks)* is moved from its usual location, files on a copied disk will be inaccessible; the instructions telling the computer where the directory is cannot be copied by normal copy commands.

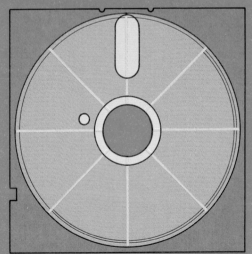

Instead of using standard copy commands, a programmer could instruct the computer to copy data from one disk to another by naming sector and track coordinates. Activating these commands requires that the pirate be well versed in the computer's operating system.

system in Maryland. A little more than two years earlier, county officials had purchased from a California-based company a new, computerized circulation system to help librarians check books in and out, keep track of overdue volumes and perform a miscellany of other circulation chores.

The system cost $900,000, and the librarians were unhappy with it from the first day of operation, in June 1980, primarily because it ran much more slowly than promised. It took an agonizing 4.9 seconds to check a book in and 6.4 seconds to check one out; neither task should have taken more than two seconds. The California firm tried to improve the system's speed in 1981, but the results failed to satisfy the terms of the contract. In frustration, county officials refused to pay the $218,000 balance due until the system functioned as promised.

Later that year, according to the assistant county attorney, an official at the company in California responded with a veiled threat: If the county failed to pay in full, "there was something in the system that would shut it down." With the guidance of a local computer expert, the library's systems manager began searching for that something and found it hidden in the program early in 1982.

Altered checksums. Checksums, results of mathematical operations on the bits in a sector, are used to verify accuracy when a disk is used. Incorrect checksums are put in some sectors of protected software; instructions stop operations if the errors are corrected, as occurs when a disk is copied.

Half tracks. Some systems use so-called half tracks between the tracks a disk drive usually reads or writes data on. A program on the half tracks *(below, red)* must also have instructions (which cannot be copied with standard commands) telling the computer how to reposition the drive heads.

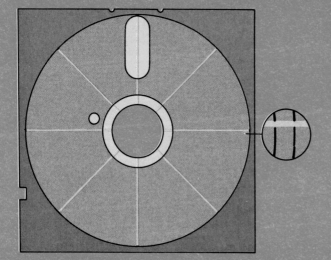

A pirate who can program in low-level assembly language can remove the instructions to look for incorrect checksums or write instructions telling the computer to copy the disk exactly, errors and all.

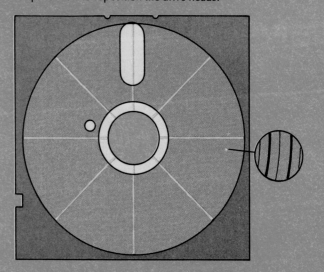

Circumventing this protection method requires programming expertise. A pirate who is familiar with both assembly language and the workings of disk-drive hardware can write a program to reposition the drive heads to read the copied disk.

It was a logic bomb timed to go off on March 15—just a couple of weeks later.

Without telling the California firm that the logic bomb had been pinpointed, the county attorney telegraphed a warning: If the system failed, the Californians would be held liable. In response, the firm sent a program segment ostensibly to disarm the bomb. But the new instructions for the computer only rescheduled the detonation date, moving it five months into the future. Exasperated county programmers could not remove the bad instructions altogether for fear of introducing other errors into the system, so they disabled the bomb by resetting the date to 1999, long after the computer's scheduled retirement. In the end, the contract was taken over by the California firm's bonding agent, which, in an ironic twist, hired the firm to fix the county's system. After successful tests in October 1983, more than three years from the date the system first went into operation, the county paid its balance due—to the bonding company.

Programs like the library logic bomb cause trouble enough by attacking one computer system at a time. The potential harm increases exponentially, however, in the case of software that is designed to spread from one computer to

Ambiguous bits. A disk may be physically altered so that the computer reads designated bits sometimes as ones, sometimes as zeros. A normal copy program cannot reproduce these ambiguous bits; it writes a one or a zero. Software can be designed not to work if ambiguous bits are missing.

Hardware key. One way to protect a program is to put only part of it on a disk, and the rest into a microchip that plugs into the computer through a connecting device. The chip and the device act like a key to unlock the software; without it, the program on a pirated disk will not run.

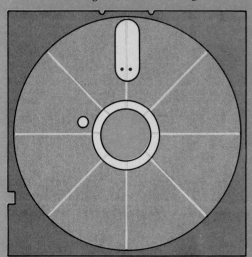

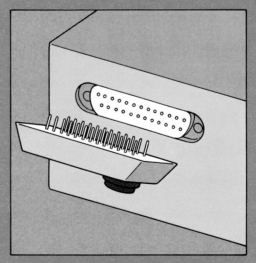

As with most other copy-protection methods, one way to bypass this scheme is to manipulate the original program at the assembly-language level, removing the instructions that tell the computer to look for ambiguous bits in the first place.

Dividing a program between a disk and a chip might stymie some copiers, but determined software pirates working in assembly language could eventually program their way around this protection system.

another. Programs called worms, for instance, can burrow through networks to lodge in other computers.

The worm was invented as an experiment in 1980 by John Schoch and Jon Hupp of the Xerox Corporation's Palo Alto Research Center in California. Schoch and Hupp hoped that such programs could take over a variety of network chores. One of their worms wriggled through large networks looking for idle computers and harnessing their power to help solve big problems. Another searched for—and reported—computer malfunctions. In the hands of a less responsible programmer, however, an unauthorized worm program can wreak havoc.

A WORM RUN AMUCK

On Wednesday evening, November 2, 1988, just such a renegade worm entered Internet, a system that links hundreds of computer networks joining more than 60,000 computers. Within hours, the worm had slowed thousands of those machines to a halt at sites that included M.I.T., the University of California at Berkeley, three NASA facilities, Los Alamos and Lawrence Livermore national laboratories, the Rand Corporation and SRI International.

Programmers at several universities worked through the night to analyze and contain the invader, issuing the first anti-worm tactics before dawn. By the weekend, network managers had all but eradicated the rogue program. It had done no permanent damage to stored files or programs, but its disruptive spread had cost hundreds of hours of human effort and computer time.

The computer-science grapevine soon identified the worm's author: 23-year-old Robert Tappan Morris, a Cornell graduate student. Ironically, he was the son of Robert Morris, a computer-security expert at the ultra-secret National Security Agency. The younger Morris remained in seclusion, but his friends talked freely to the press. According to their account, Morris had intended his worm as a harmless program that would place single copies of itself in Internet computers by exploiting flaws in network software. The worm had no purpose, they said, other than to show off its author's expertise. But like a latter-day sorcerer's apprentice, Morris made a mistake. A programming error prevented the worm from recognizing which computers it had already infiltrated, so that it repeatedly planted copies of itself in the same machines. Soon the computers overloaded with hundreds or thousands of worm replicas, all actively at work searching for new hosts to invade.

Whether or not his friends were right about his motives, Morris was convicted in 1990 under the Federal Computer Fraud and Abuse Act of 1986 and sentenced to 400 hours of community service, three years of probation, and a $10,000 fine.

As for Internet, network members and software suppliers patched the holes through which the worm had passed but did little else to improve security. As a Cornell committee on the worm incident put it, "A community of scholars should not have to build walls as high as the sky to achieve privacy, particularly when such walls impede the free flow of information." Besides, their report admitted, "to build such walls would be futile in a community of individuals with the knowledge and skills required to scale the highest barriers."

The Morris case, though sensational, was a rarity, the first documented instance of an unauthorized worm on a major network. Far more common—and often more destructive—are intruders known as viruses. Unlike a worm, a virus is only a fragment of a program and cannot run independently. Instead, a virus gets into a computer by attaching to a program such as a spreadsheet or a word processor. When the host program is activated, the virus enters the computer's memory. There it attaches copies of itself to other software. The contaminated programs may then infect software in any computer that uses them, spreading the virus like an epidemic. What happens next depends on the virus. Some do nothing more than display a mischievous message. Others are programmed like logic bombs to wait for a certain date and then delete every file in active use. Still another variety counts the disks to which it spreads and erases, for example, every fifth disk.

In 1984, Fred Cohen, then a researcher at the University of Southern California, sounded a virus alarm. He told a conference on computer security of an experiment during which a virus he had created was able to infect an intensively used computer network in a period as short as five minutes. In another experiment, he showed that even an operating system designed to satisfy requirements for military security can be vulnerable to viruses.

Cohen issued his initial alert with minicomputers and mainframes in mind, but the chief target of actual viruses has been the personal computer. Scores was one such virus. Designed to attack microcomputers in the Apple Macintosh family, Scores first appeared in September 1987 in Dallas, Texas, at Electronic Data Systems (EDS), an information-processing firm. The virus, judging from its coded instructions, was intended to search for and sabotage certain customized EDS programs. Although intended as harmless to any other software, Scores, simply by entering a Macintosh, interfered with the computer's operating system and created a host of unintended symptoms. Victims reported printers that wouldn't print, software that ran slowly and other programs that simply stopped dead—with the loss of all recently entered data.

Spreading outward from EDS on shared floppy disks, Scores eventually infected more than 14,000 Macintosh computers in homes and businesses throughout North America. In May 1988, a concerned Apple Computer Company began distributing VIRUS RX, a free program to detect and eliminate Scores and other viruses. Even so, isolated Scores cases continued to bedevil Macintosh users for more than a year.

VIRUS RX is one of dozens of anti-viral programs known as vaccines. Some vaccines watch for—and halt—suspicious activities, such as attempts to rewrite parts of the operating system; others cure diseased computers by ferreting out and deleting infected files. Since viruses vary considerably, however, even the best vaccine will combat only those types it is designed to detect. For the best protection, experts stress two precautions: wariness in acquiring new programs of uncertain provenance; and routine archiving, or backup, of programs and data. Files lost to a viral assault can be recovered from the spare copies.

A BATTERY OF DEFENSIVE WEAPONS

Regular backups, which also guard against accidental erasures, are fundamental to any computer security scheme. But the task of copying files can be so tedious that computer users often postpone or avoid it. A more reliable solution is an automated backup system requiring no human intervention. Other schemes enable computers to protect themselves by a variety of methods. Appropriately equipped and programmed, a computer system can stand guard to keep outsiders such as hackers from getting in. It can segregate sensitive files and programs to prevent access by unauthorized employees. It can encrypt data, rendering it unreadable to anyone not having the secret key that unlocks the meaning *(Chapter 4)*. And if all else has failed, the computer assumes the role of detective, helping to track down the culprit who has compromised the system.

Taken together, such computer-protection measures are costly. Consequently, most computer systems rely on a single access-control method to ensure that only authorized users are allowed to log onto, or enter, a system. Of all the options, passwords are most widely used. They have served as computer guardians since the rise of time-sharing systems in the late 1960s. In allowing simultaneous use of the computer by many people, time sharing necessitated some method of ensuring that only authorized persons had access to certain programs and information. Later, passwords also became the method of choice for verifying the identity of individuals logging onto computer networks linked by telephone.

The effectiveness of passwords hinges on the challenging task of keeping them

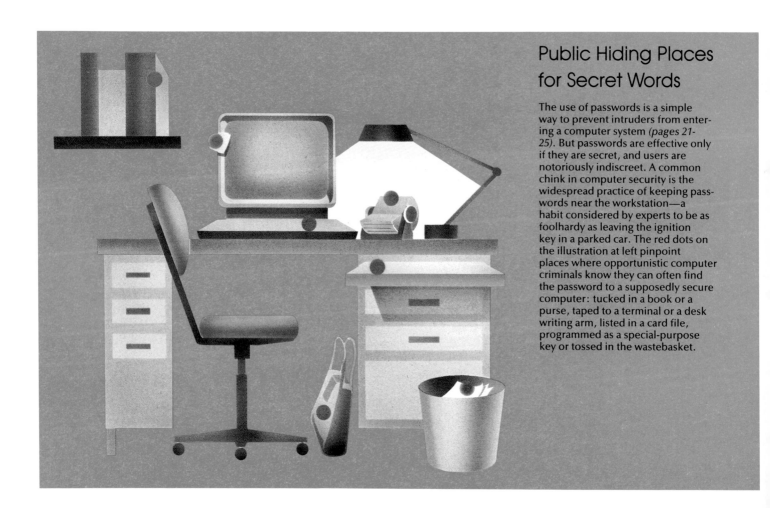

Public Hiding Places for Secret Words

The use of passwords is a simple way to prevent intruders from entering a computer system *(pages 21-25)*. But passwords are effective only if they are secret, and users are notoriously indiscreet. A common chink in computer security is the widespread practice of keeping passwords near the workstation—a habit considered by experts to be as foolhardy as leaving the ignition key in a parked car. The red dots on the illustration at left pinpoint places where opportunistic computer criminals know they can often find the password to a supposedly secure computer: tucked in a book or a purse, taped to a terminal or a desk writing arm, listed in a card file, programmed as a special-purpose key or tossed in the wastebasket.

secret. Obstacles to secrecy abound. For example, people tend to choose passwords meaningful in their own lives, such as a social security number or the name of a spouse or a pet. But these choices, tricky as they may seem to someone selecting a password, are among the first possibilities that any intruder would try.

So many passwords fall short of the ideal that computer-system managers often find it simpler to protect inferior passwords from discovery than to try to enforce the selection of secure passwords. One effective tactic is to program the computer to alert human watchdogs in response to repeated guesses at passwords. As an aid to tracking down those who have broken through the computer's defenses, many operating systems maintain an audit trail, a record of computer activity that includes all attempts to gain access to the system.

But if the intruder succeeds in getting past the barriers, any record of the intrusion may simply disappear; programmers can easily write a Trojan horse that covers their tracks. Furthermore, hackers have been known to contrive trap doors and Trojan horse attacks to obtain the master list of passwords stored in the computer or even to bypass the normal log-on procedure altogether.

A PROTECTIVE ANSWERING MACHINE
Computers and operating systems offer varying degrees of password protection and audit trails, and some give no such safeguards at all. One piece of hardware than can fill this security gap is a port protection device (PPD). The size of a cigar box and containing its own microprocessor and memory, a PPD is a kind of super answering machine installed between the phone line and the socket, or port, where the modem plugs into the host computer. A PPD answers the telephone and insists on a valid password before connecting a caller to the computer. PPDs can confuse the uninitiated with a variety of smokescreens. Some models hide the computer's identity by answering the phone with a synthesized human voice instead of the distinctive tone issued when a computer answers. Others, instead of prompting the caller to log on, offer no clue how to proceed. Only users who have been taught the correct response are likely to be connected to the computer.

Many PPDs provide a so-called event log, a record of activity that can serve as an audit trail, and some include a clever security feature known as a call-back device. After verifying a valid password, the machine hangs up and checks its internal memory for the telephone number of the authorized user who was assigned the password. Then it dials that number to make certain the log-on attempt originated there. In response, the authorized user must enter an access code before the connection to the host computer is made.

PPDs have some disadvantages. They slow the log-on process for legitimate users of the system and, in the call-back versions, run up the host computer's telephone bill, since the call that ultimately allows access originates there. Moreover, some hackers insist that, with their intimate knowledge of telephone call-forwarding technology, they can circumvent the devices by arranging to have the machine's return call automatically switched to another number.

Thus the battle waxes and wanes. Each remedy that security experts propose seems to bear the seeds of the countermeasures that will be used against it. The only way to ensure the safety and integrity of a computer system is to isolate it. The United States' armed forces restrict access to some computers that handle top-secret information in just that way, shutting them off in heavily guarded, vaultlike rooms. Few people may enter, and there is no provision for using the computer from a remote location except by dedicated telephone lines that outsiders cannot dial into and that are difficult to tap. For civilians, such a solution would be a throwback to the early days of computers, when huge machines sat in isolation, communicating only with their immediate attendants. Indeed, closing off the computer would defeat the very purpose of time-sharing and telephone-linked systems, which exist to make the power of the computer conveniently available to as many authorized users as possible.

WITH FRIENDS LIKE THESE . . .

Even such stringent precautions are not foolproof; there remains the possibility that a computer's defenses against outsiders can be made irrelevant by what security consultant Robert Courtney has called "a Trojan horse of a different kind"—a treacherous employee. But even insiders can be thwarted in many of their schemes by the computer itself, if it contains sentinels built into the operating system that manages all of the machine's resources.

Like the use of passwords, the operating system's role as an internal guardian dates from the early evolution of time sharing. Time sharing required the operating system to juggle several programs and users simultaneously. The programmers who made it possible had to develop ways to segregate programs and data files in order to prevent them from interfering with one another and with the operating system itself.

From these needs evolved a generation of large-computer operating systems that compartmentalize data and software. This partitioning makes possible built-in security based on the user's need to know or to work with a given set of data. A secretary in marketing, for example, might be allowed access to computer files relevant to that department, but might be denied the privilege of running programs or seeing data concerned with another department, such as payroll. Such schemes, as well as other security measures, were codified by the National Security Agency in a 1983 publication nicknamed the Orange Book for its distinctive cover. The Orange Book, which is used to evaluate most federal and some commercial networks, describes levels of operating-system security ranging from D (incomplete) to a near-perfect A1. Systems at the B or A level—and many of those rated C—maintain a strict hierarchy of user privilege not unlike the layers of security classification used by the military. One method for enforcing this hierarchy of privileged use is the reference monitor—a tamperproof kernel of software that checks the legitimacy of every attempt to gain access to data or programs (pages 82-83).

Yet even a reference-monitor type of operating system must provide for access by at least a handful of the most trustworthy programmers and system analysts, the very people most capable of uncovering and exploiting flaws in security. Two eminent Dutch security researchers, I. S. Herschberg and Ronald Paans, have written of this irony: "Whoever permits programming to be done on his system has, by this very permission, lost his system. Every programmer constitutes a threat. Tragically, programmers are more threatening in direct proportion to their qualities as programmers. A crack programmer implicitly is a cracksman." Said another authority: "Telling a programmer that a computer system is safe from penetration is like waving a red flag in front of a bull."

Thwarting
an Inside Job

3

In the war of wits between computer-security experts and would-be electronic intruders, the focus is frequently internal. Multi-user computer systems often place parts of the system off limits to certain users: For example, many of the system's users may be allowed to do general work such as word processing or graphics design, whereas only a few may be allowed to modify or even view files containing payroll information or other sensitive data.

Two basic approaches to preventing internal trespass are explained on the following pages. Both methods make use of the computer's operating system, the set of programs that acts as the intermediary between the user and the machine, allocating access to shared resources such as printers and providing the framework within which every other program carries out its assigned tasks. One of the operating system's primary functions is to keep track of the location of all files (which may be in storage on disk or tape or may reside temporarily in the computer's memory); the job makes the operating system well suited to controlling who can see files or alter them.

In one method of governing internal access to files, the rules are rather simple and are attached to the files themselves. The operating system simply determines whether or not users are allowed to see a file at all and, if so, whether they are allowed to make alterations to it.

In the second type of setup, more stringent rules are built into a special portion of the operating system called a reference monitor (pages 82-85). The second approach can thwart a form of electronic attack called a Trojan horse. Such a software ploy—every bit as insidious as the wooden horse that smuggled Greek warriors through the gates of Troy in Homer's *Iliad*—appears innocuous or even helpful. But unless the right kind of security barriers are in place, it can send confidential data to prying eyes at electronic speed.

Gaining Admission to a Multi-User System

In most large multi-user computer systems, everyone who wishes to work on the computer, whether to type a memo or to enter new information into an existing data base, must first go through a start-up procedure called logging on or logging in, regardless of any security measures that may come into play later. The procedure, controlled by a program in the computer's operating system, either confirms a user's identity and attendant rights to enter the system, or denies access to an

To log onto his company's multi-user computer system, Bob, a salesperson, types his name at the keyboard of his terminal. This signals the operating system that he wants access to the computer. The operating system fetches the names-and-passwords file into temporary memory, finds Bob's name as an authorized user, and displays a password request. When Bob types in his secret password, the operating system determines that it matches the one on file with Bob's name, and he is given access to the system.

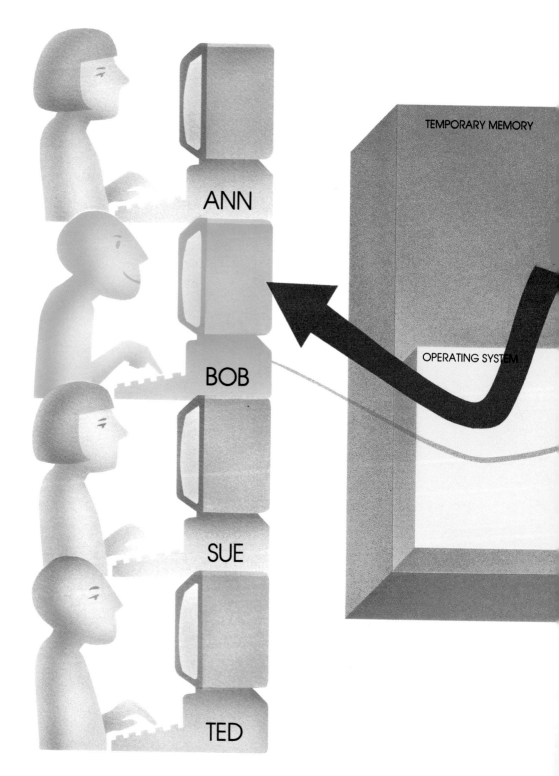

TEMPORARY MEMORY

OPERATING SYSTEM

ANN

BOB

SUE

TED

unauthorized person. Not only does the log-on procedure screen would-be users on the premises, it can also foil automated long-distance hacker attacks by rigorously limiting the number of unsuccessful attempts permitted per telephone call *(page 21)*.

In the sample system shown here and on the following pages, four employees are entitled to varying degrees of access to their company's computer system. In order for them to be able to operate such workday applications as the text-edit program, for instance, or to take a look at specific data, they must call that program or data file from storage on a tape or disk into the computer's temporary memory. All such requests for computerized files are made by way of the operating system, which will carry out only those requests made by users whose identity has been established during the log-on procedure.

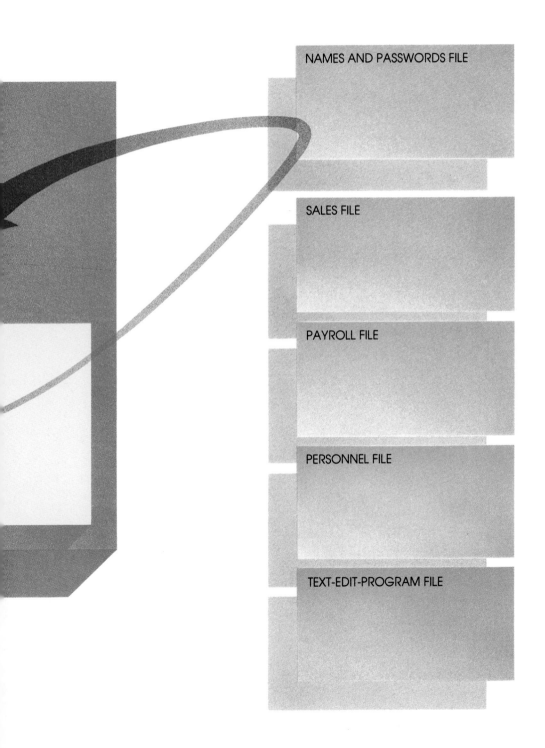

NAMES AND PASSWORDS FILE

SALES FILE

PAYROLL FILE

PERSONNEL FILE

TEXT-EDIT-PROGRAM FILE

Controlling Access to Computer Files

A simple method of regulating the security of electronic files is to head each one with a kind of shield known as an access-control list (ACL). An ACL names those authorized to use a file and specifies what kind of access each person is permitted. So-called read-access allows an individual to use a program or to look at the contents of a file but does not grant the right to alter the program or file in any way; to make additions, deletions or other changes, a user must also have write-access.

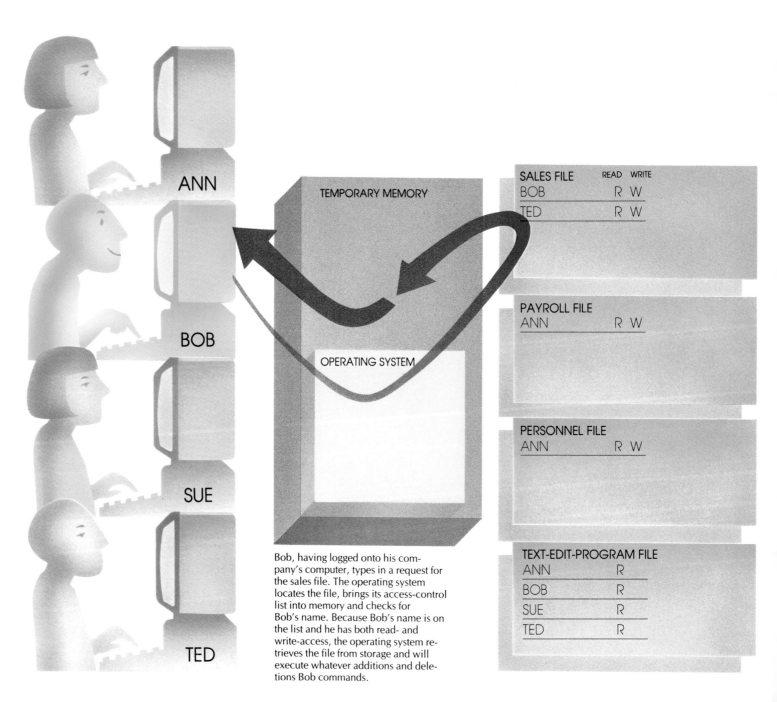

ANN

BOB

SUE

TED

TEMPORARY MEMORY

OPERATING SYSTEM

SALES FILE	READ	WRITE
BOB	R	W
TED	R	W

PAYROLL FILE		
ANN	R	W

PERSONNEL FILE		
ANN	R	W

TEXT-EDIT-PROGRAM FILE	
ANN	R
BOB	R
SUE	R
TED	R

Bob, having logged onto his company's computer, types in a request for the sales file. The operating system locates the file, brings its access-control list into memory and checks for Bob's name. Because Bob's name is on the list and he has both read- and write-access, the operating system retrieves the file from storage and will execute whatever additions and deletions Bob commands.

When the operating system receives a request for a file, it must first bring the relevant ACL into temporary memory to check for the user's name; only if the name is found will the file itself be brought into memory.

As indicated by the ACLs of the sample files below, an employee's access varies from file to file. Ann, a high-level executive, has both read- and write-access to the payroll and personnel files, allowing her the ability to add bonuses or adjust salaries. (Company accountants, on the other hand, might be given only read-access, allowing them merely to audit payroll records.) Salesperson Bob and sales manager Ted each have both read- and write-access to the sales file; either of them can update those records. Sue, the company secretary, has not been given access to any of the data files but does have read-access to the text-edit-program file for word processing, as does everyone else.

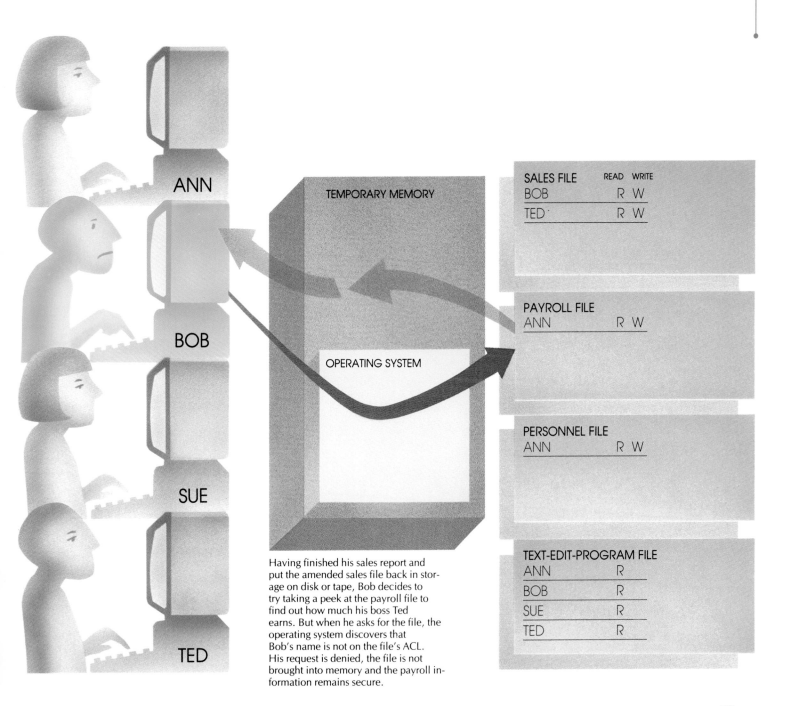

ANN

BOB

SUE

TED

TEMPORARY MEMORY

OPERATING SYSTEM

Having finished his sales report and put the amended sales file back in storage on disk or tape, Bob decides to try taking a peek at the payroll file to find out how much his boss Ted earns. But when he asks for the file, the operating system discovers that Bob's name is not on the file's ACL. His request is denied, the file is not brought into memory and the payroll information remains secure.

SALES FILE	READ	WRITE
BOB	R	W
TED	R	W

PAYROLL FILE		
ANN	R	W

PERSONNEL FILE		
ANN	R	W

TEXT-EDIT-PROGRAM FILE		
ANN	R	
BOB	R	
SUE	R	
TED	R	

Sneaking Data
from Restricted Files

A system that relies principally on access-control lists for security can provide an effective safeguard against casual attempts to enter sensitive files. However, an ACL security system is vulnerable to a Trojan horse, a seemingly innocent piece of software that conceals within its code malicious instructions that deceive the computer and cause it to open confidential files. To carry out a Trojan horse attack, an unauthorized user first buries a request for restricted data inside some other program. The would-be trespasser then induces an authorized user to run the program and—all unknowingly—activate the request for restricted data. Shown below are the steps Bob undertakes to prepare a Trojan horse invasion of the payroll file.

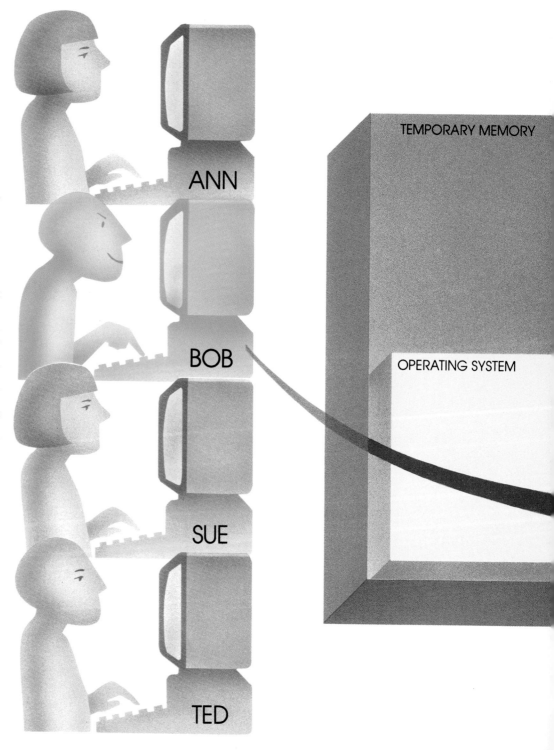

To build a Trojan horse, Bob first creates two new files, Bob's text-edit file and Bob's secret file, heading each one with an ACL that gives him both read- and write-access (1). He also gives Ann, who has access to the payroll file, read-access to Bob's text-edit file and write-access to Bob's secret file. Next, Bob copies the company's text-edit-program file into Bob's text-edit file (2): His read-access to the text-edit program allows him to copy it.

Because he has given himself write-access to the new file, Bob is now free to alter the copy. He writes two new sets of instructions (3). The first set automatically adjusts each page of text to make room for footnotes—a helpful feature designed to entice Ann into using the altered program. The second set of instructions is the secret one: It amends the text-edit program so that as soon as Ann activates it, the operating system will be asked to copy the payroll file into Bob's secret file.

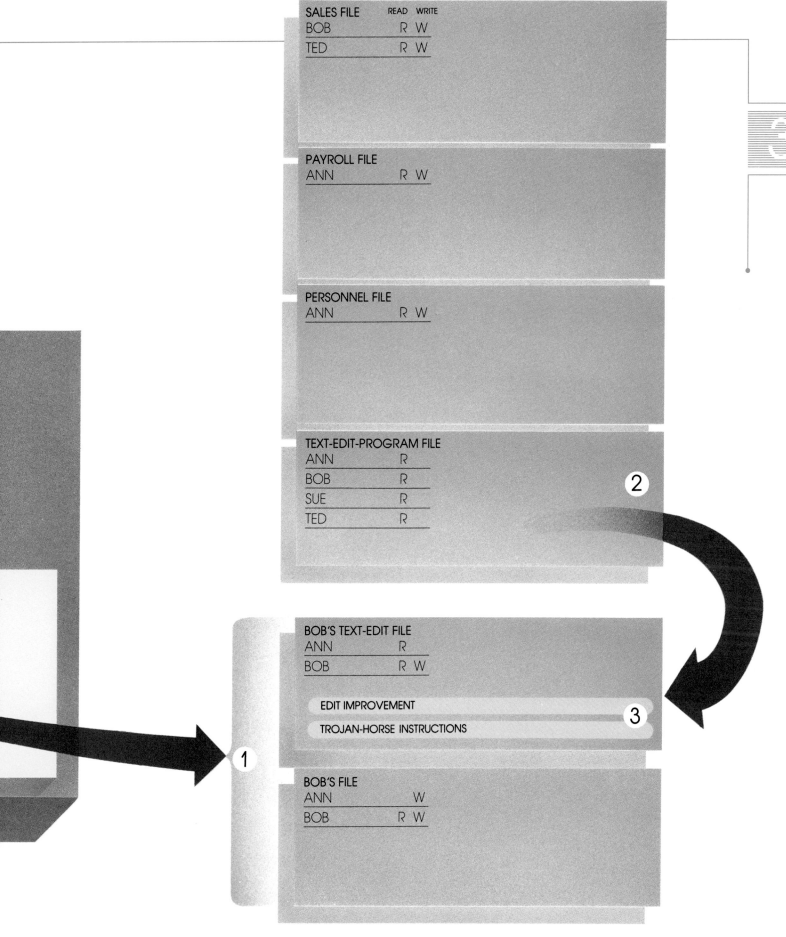

SALES FILE

	READ	WRITE
BOB	R	W
TED	R	W

PAYROLL FILE

ANN	R	W

PERSONNEL FILE

ANN	R	W

TEXT-EDIT-PROGRAM FILE

ANN	R
BOB	R
SUE	R
TED	R

BOB'S TEXT-EDIT FILE

ANN	R
BOB	R W

EDIT IMPROVEMENT

TROJAN-HORSE INSTRUCTIONS

BOB'S FILE

ANN	W
BOB	R W

To put his Trojan horse into action, Bob shows Ann the new footnote feature in the word-processing program he has stored as Bob's text-edit file and convinces her that it is an improvement over the company's version.

Ann requests Bob's program the next time she does word processing; since she has been given read-access to the file, the operating system complies. Ann uses the new program, unaware that she is activating the Trojan horse and telling the computer to copy the restricted payroll file into Bob's newly created secret file, which he can read at will.

Such a command from Bob would be refused; but Ann, who seems to be making the request, has read-access to the payroll file, so the operating system perceives the command as legitimate.

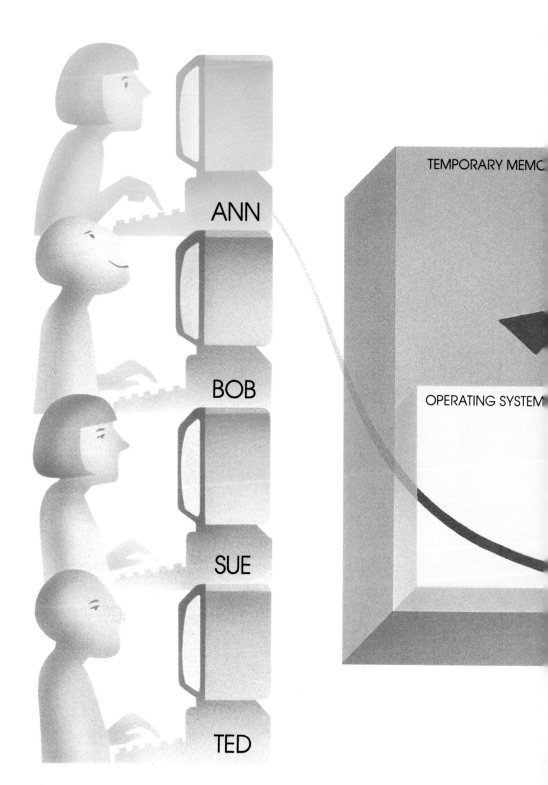

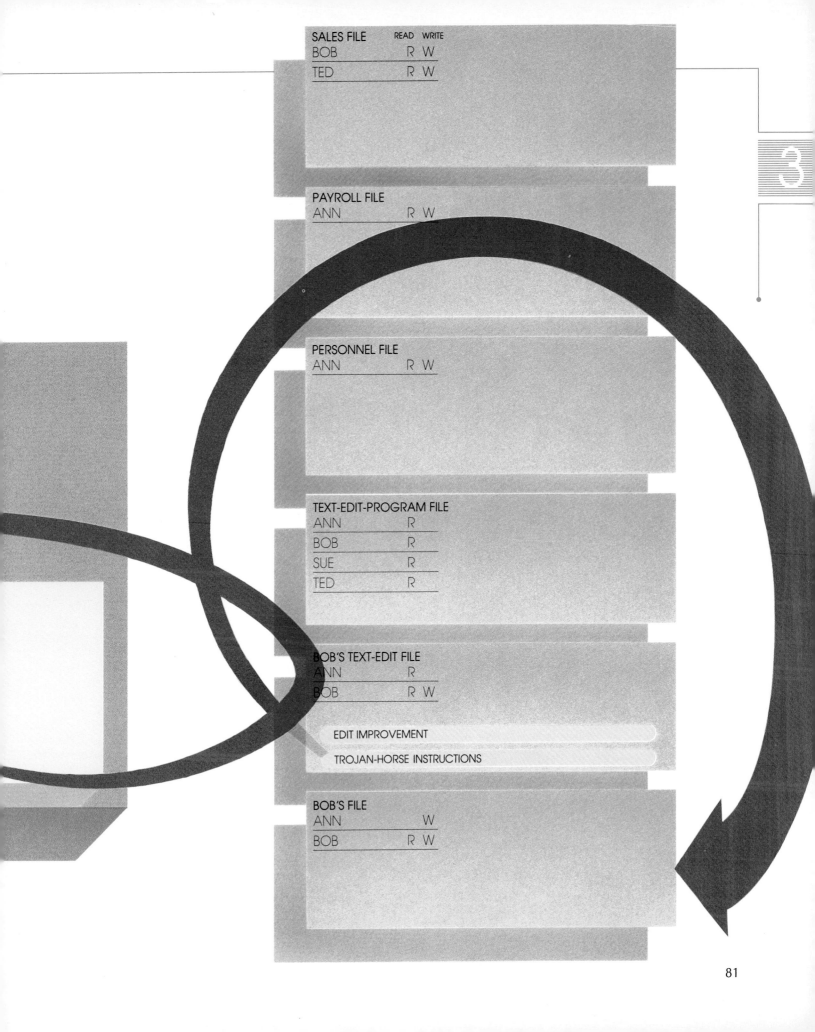

SALES FILE · READ · WRITE
BOB · R · W
TED · R · W

PAYROLL FILE
ANN · R · W

PERSONNEL FILE
ANN · R · W

TEXT-EDIT-PROGRAM FILE
ANN · R
BOB · R
SUE · R
TED · R

BOB'S TEXT-EDIT FILE
ANN · R
BOB · R · W

EDIT IMPROVEMENT

TROJAN-HORSE INSTRUCTIONS

BOB'S FILE
ANN · W
BOB · R · W

Erecting a Barrier against a Trojan Horse

One of the best defenses against a software Trojan horse is a set of operating-system programs known collectively as a reference monitor. A reference monitor defines each request for access as a reference to a specific file and, as shown on the following two pages, monitors all references by subjecting them to a strict protocol.

Reference monitors may be designed in a variety of ways, but each places a filter between users and stored computer files; the filter must be tamperproof but simple enough to allow system designers to test it. Generally, reference monitors work by assigning each file and each user a security classification. Files and users may be divided into only two categories, classified and unclassified, or they may be ranked in a hierarchy of security levels like that employed by governments to classify state secrets and military information.

In the system shown here, the reference monitor consists of a two-part filter. The first part contains two rules that apply to all users. According to Rule 1, users may read only those files at or below their own security classification; they may not see files classified at a higher level. Rule 2 forbids users to write into files below their own level, blocking any flow of classified information into less secure files. If a user's request for access to a file passes the tests in the first part of the filter, it is then tested against a file-user list to satisfy the second part; the list contains the names of all files and their authorized users, specifying read-access, write-access or both. If a user asks to see a file above his or her classification, the request will not only be refused, but also noted in a confidential file accessible only to the security officer.

A reference monitor does have an Achilles' heel: The system does not foil a Trojan horse if the electronic burglar happens to have a security classification matching that of the file being stolen. However, because a reference-monitor system may employ numerous security levels, authorized users at a given classification may be few indeed—severely limiting the number of suspects in the event of a security breach.

TEMP

OPER

The four users shown here and on the following two pages have been divided into two color-coded security levels: pink for access to classified files, purple for unclassified files. In practice, most reference-monitor systems would employ many more levels of security classification.

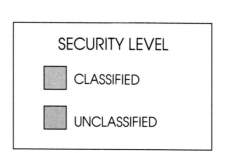

SECURITY LEVEL

CLASSIFIED

UNCLASSIFIED

REFERENCE MONITOR

1

Rule One:
Cannot read
a higher
classification

2

Rule Two:
Cannot write
to a lower
classification

SALES	READ	WRITE
BOB	R	W
TED	R	W

PAYROLL		
ANN	R	W

PERSONNEL		
ANN	R	W

TEXT-EDIT PROGRAM		
ANN	R	
BOB	R	
SUE	R	
TED	R	

BOB'S TEXT EDIT		
ANN	R	
BOB	R	W

BOB'S FILE		
ANN		W
BOB	R	W

SALES FILE	READ	WRITE
BOB	R	W
TED	R	W

PAYROLL FILE		
ANN	R	W

PERSONNEL FILE		
ANN	R	W

TEXT-EDIT-PROGRAM FILE		
ANN	R	
BOB	R	
SUE	R	
TED	R	

BOB'S TEXT-EDIT FILE		
ANN	R	
BOB	R	W

BOB'S FILE		
ANN		W
BOB	R	W

File requests must pass through a two-part filter. The first part, consisting of two rules, screens out requests to read higher-level files (Rule 1) and blocks attempts to write into lower-level files (Rule 2). A request that survives the first part of the filter is then tested against the file-user list in the second part.

Like the users in this example, files are also divided into two color-coded security levels: pink for classified, purple for unclassified. None of the files is headed by an access-control list; rather, all access-control information is contained in the reference monitor.

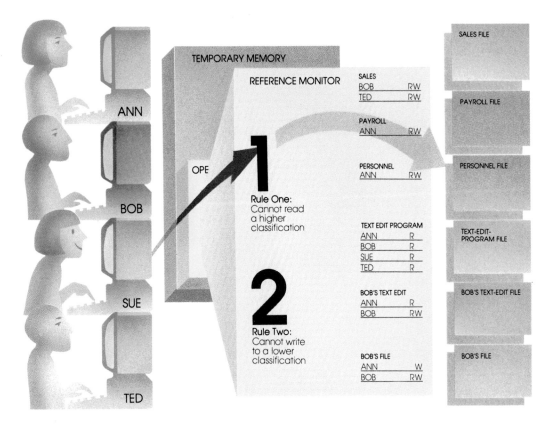

In this example, the operating system's reference monitor stops unauthorized access at the first checkpoint when Sue, the company secretary, types in a request to read the classified personnel file. The program compares Sue's classification with that of the personnel file, sees that she is asking to read a file above her security level, and applies Rule 1 to deny her access.

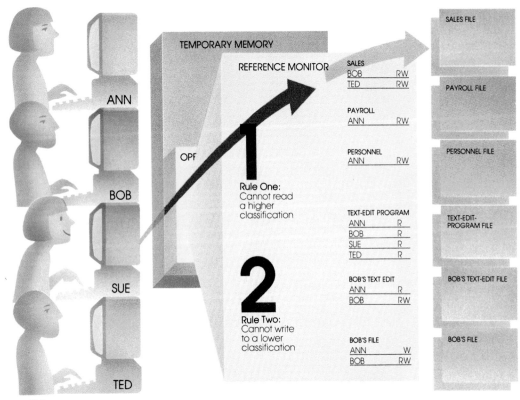

Next, Sue asks to read the sales file. This request gets through the first part of the reference-monitor filter: The file's classification is not higher than Sue's, so her request is legitimate under Rule 1. Then the operating system checks the file-user list to see if Sue has been granted access to that particular unclassified file. Her name is not on the list, so access is denied.

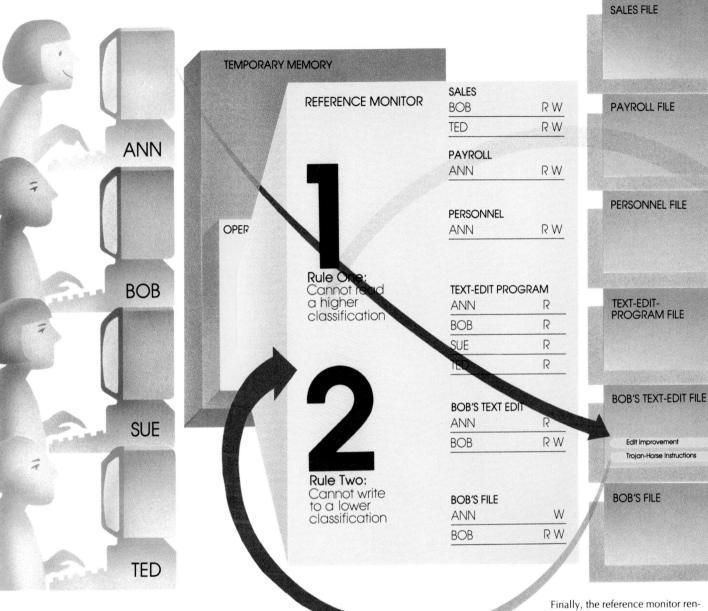

TEMPORARY MEMORY

REFERENCE MONITOR

OPER

1

Rule One:
Cannot read
a higher
classification

2

Rule Two:
Cannot write
to a lower
classification

SALES		
BOB	R	W
TED	R	W

PAYROLL		
ANN	R	W

PERSONNEL		
ANN	R	W

TEXT-EDIT PROGRAM	
ANN	R
BOB	R
SUE	R
TED	R

BOB'S TEXT EDIT		
ANN	R	
BOB	R	W

BOB'S FILE		
ANN		W
BOB	R	W

SALES FILE

PAYROLL FILE

PERSONNEL FILE

TEXT-EDIT-
PROGRAM FILE

BOB'S TEXT-EDIT FILE

Edit Improvement

Trojan-Horse Instructions

BOB'S FILE

ANN

BOB

SUE

TED

Finally, the reference monitor renders the computer's classified files impervious to Bob's Trojan horse attack. Bob can create his trick files as before, and Ann can use his altered word-processing program, since Rule 1 grants her read-access to lower-level files. But when Ann unknowingly activates Bob's hidden instructions to copy the classified payroll file into Bob's unclassified file, Rule 2 goes into action. Because Rule 2 prohibits Ann from writing information into a file with a lower security level than her own, Bob's Trojan horse is blocked at the gate.

Impenetrable Ciphers

Near Culpeper, Virginia, in the farming and horse-raising country southwest of Washington, D.C., stands an unimposing two-story building constructed of concrete block. A no-trespassing sign dissuades the casually curious from stepping beyond the decorative wood-rail fence that surrounds the structure, but visitors are not challenged until they reach the door. There, guards posted inside scrutinize them over closed-circuit television before granting admission.

Security is tight here because vast fortunes pass through the building each day. Yet the amount of cash on hand rarely exceeds the sum of whatever money the employees may have in their pockets and purses. The facility belongs to S.W.I.F.T., the Society for Worldwide Interbank Financial Telecommunications. Headquartered in Belgium, S.W.I.F.T. exists solely to provide electronic-funds-transfer (EFT) services to banks and other financial institutions. S.W.I.F.T. processes in excess of a million transactions daily for more than 2,300 banks in 56 countries, and all without the exchange of a single piece of paper—not a bank note, not a check, not a deposit or withdrawal slip.

These transactions take the form of computer-generated payment messages that are transmitted by means of a modem connected to each network terminal. A member bank in the United States, for example, may be instructed to credit the account of a corporation in Germany with so many million dollars and debit a company in Singapore for the same amount.

As long as the messages remain within S.W.I.F.T.'s operations centers, they are safe. But as soon as they are transmitted to race along telephone wires, they become vulnerable. Unless special measures are taken, a modern Dalton Gang armed with computer and modem could intercept the payment instructions, then modify them so that the funds would be deposited in the gang's account instead of in the rightful one. Or an international terrorist could introduce spurious messages designed to throw the world financial system into chaos.

Yet such scenarios are highly unlikely, largely because of the form in which S.W.I.F.T. and other international networks transfer assets electronically. Before transmission, the contents of each payment message are scrambled by a combination of special computer hardware and software so that even a supremely brilliant and dedicated cryptanalyst equipped with a powerful computer would require more than a lifetime to extract the meaning.

S.W.I.F.T.'s encryption system is designed to forestall the kind of surreptitious holdups that have enriched the unscrupulous and made victims of computerized financial institutions since the middle of the 1970s. For example, an ingenious Japanese engineer, armed with a tape recorder and an oscilloscope, tapped into the telephone system at the Hokkaido Bank and intercepted messages coming from automatic teller machines (ATMs) to the bank's central computer. From these communications, he copied customer names and identification numbers onto magnetic identification cards and used the cards to withdraw from ATMs 1.33 million yen (about $6,500) that belonged to other people. Thanks prima-

Data traveling between computers is vulnerable to interception by eavesdroppers. Encryption renders their efforts fruitless by rearranging the data into a jumble that makes no sense to anyone who does not possess the secret key needed to decipher it.

rily to encipherment, S.W.I.F.T. has evaded such costly embarrassments.

Increasingly in today's new era of computer insecurity, not only banks but also other businesses and government agencies are turning to encryption. Computer-security experts consider it the best and most practical way to protect computer data from unauthorized disclosure when transmitted and even when stored on disk, tape or the magnetic strip of a credit card.

AN ANCIENT ART

Such applications highlight a change for ciphers and codes, which traditionally have been the province of war and intrigue rather than of commerce. The practice of cryptography dates from antiquity, deriving its name from the Greek roots for "hidden writing." As early as the fifth century B.C., for example, the rulers of Sparta, a militaristic Greek city-state, employed a cipher device called a scytale—from the word for "staff"—to disguise communications of an official nature. The scytale consisted of a baton with a long strip of parchment wrapped spirally around it.

A Spartan ruler lettered his message along the length of the baton. Then he unwrapped the parchment, thereby rendering it into a strip of unconnected characters, and sent the encrypted message off by courier. An enemy who captured the parchment would find only a meaningless jumble. The message could be deciphered only by someone who had the key: a baton of identical diameter. When the parchment was wound on this baton, the words leaped forth.

The scytale is the first known use of transposition, a classic encryption technique. Also called permutation, transposition rearranges the order of the characters in a message. The Roman emperor Julius Caesar, who conquered much of Europe and the Middle East, encrypted confidential correspondence with a different technique, one called substitution. He replaced each letter of a message with one taken from a position further along in the alphabet. For example, if Caesar chose to use letters three places removed from the original, for every a that appeared in his message, he substituted the letter d in the encryption. At the end of the alphabet, y became a b, and so on.

Caesar's process of substituting one letter for another and the Spartans' practice of reordering the letters of a message are both examples of what modern cryptologists call an algorithm—a procedure or set of rules for accomplishing something. In this case, the result is a cipher. The precise place from which the letter was taken—or in the case of the scytale, the exact diameter of the baton—is known as the key to the cipher. Without the key, the recipient could not read the message.

Understandably, the keys and their method of use were closely guarded secrets; if either or both were discovered, secrecy was lost. However, neither method offered much protection. Someone who knew the relative frequency with which letters occur in the Latin language would have had no more trouble deciphering Caesar's messages than the average newspaper reader has in puzzling out a Sunday cryptogram. The scytale required more time and effort to break than Caesar's cipher; the process was a lengthy one of trial and error in search of a baton having the correct diameter. But in the end, the scytale, too, offered only weak security. Decrypting a single word would lead quickly to the entire text of the message.

Indeed, a secure cipher is such an elusive quarry that Edgar Allan Poe, an avid amateur cryptologist who made the plot of his well-known short story "The Gold-Bug" turn upon a secret message, insisted that there can never be such a thing as an unbreakable method of encryption. "It may be roundly asserted," he maintained, "that human ingenuity cannot concoct a cipher which human ingenuity cannot resolve."

Poe was wrong, though not by much. Had Caesar randomly selected another digit—eight, for example—as the key for the second letter of his encrypted message, yet another digit for the third letter, and so on, no one except those in possession of the full sequence of numbers, or key, could have unraveled the code. By changing the number used to encrypt each letter, Caesar could have ensured the absence of any recognizable pattern that might have revealed the contents of the message. Furthermore, if he had chosen a different key for each communication, even a spy who got hold of all his messages would never have been able to decipher them.

With such a system, Caesar would have invented the so-called one-time pad, the only type of cipher that is absolutely unbreakable. In this technique, sender and receiver possess identical cipher pads. Each page contains a different key, commonly a long sequence of randomly selected digits at least as numerous as the letters in the message. A key is used to encrypt only one message, then that page is torn from the book and destroyed. From the cryptanalyst's point of view, a message encrypted with a one-time pad might mean anything, which is the same as having no meaning at all.

The one-time pad is favored for top-secret communications links, such as the Washington-Moscow hot line, where fail-safe security is necessary. But the difficulties of distributing large numbers of pads and of keeping track of each key page make the one-time pad an impractical method of encryption for widespread application.

In theory, any other encryption system can be broken. But some are superior to others, and cracking a strong cipher would require that a cryptanalyst have available unrealistically large resources in computing power. In practice, there-

fore, a code need not be unbreakable to be of use, but only so troublesome that its "work factor"—the length of time required to crack it—renders the encoded information worthless by the time it is recovered.

Cryptography remained for the most part a matter of pencil and paper until after World War I, when machines took over. Part mechanical, part electrical, these devices not only produced strong ciphers, but substantially increased the speed at which information could be encoded or decoded. One such machine, known as the Enigma, set the stage for the most celebrated code-breaking operation in history and led indirectly to the construction of the world's first large-scale digital machine.

The Enigma was invented in the early 1920s by a little-known German engineer, a Berliner named Arthur Scherbius. Intended for business use to keep confidential correspondence secret, Scherbius' device had a typewriter-like keyboard and electrical innards consisting of a maze of wires interconnecting three rotors that turned on a common shaft. The operator typed a letter of the plaintext to be encoded, and the rotors substituted a letter of ciphertext, or coded message, which lit up on a panel built into the machine. The operator then copied onto paper the letter that glowed and thus, a character at a time, encrypted the message. To decipher the message, the recipient needed an identical machine, along with a key to the initial rotor settings. Scherbius failed to convince the world of commerce that his machine merited their attention, and he died in obscurity.

But Scherbius' invention did not perish with him. When the German armies

began their sweep across Europe during the late 1930s, much of their radio traffic consisted of orders and other information encrypted on Arthur Scherbius' clever cipher device. However, Enigma's encoded messages did not fully satisfy the German high command. So the military improved the machine, adding a fourth and then a fifth rotor as well as other cipher-obscuring features. When it was finished, the Enigma was capable of scrambling a message in trillions of ways.

The British knew about Enigma, and in an attempt to master its workings, they established the code-breaking project known as *Ultra,* a name derived from the project's top-secret classification. This remarkable effort was centered at Bletchley Park, a Victorian mansion 47 miles north of London. Here, the government gathered the likes of the brilliant mathematician Alan Turing and Dillwyn Knox, a cryptanalyst who had cracked the German submarine code during World War I—while taking a bath, the story went. One writer has described the group as "a curious mixture of mathematicians, dons of various kinds, chess and crossword maestros, and an odd musician or two."

In penetrating the secrets of Enigma, Turing, Knox and their colleagues at Bletchley Park had an incalculable advantage. A replica of the machine and a description of how it worked had been smuggled out of Poland before that nation's fall in 1939. Thus forearmed, the British researchers were able to build electromechanical deciphering machines that, reversing the operation of the German device, scanned intercepted ciphertext until some linguistic pattern was discerned. Provided with such a clue, the cryptanalysts were well on the way to making sense of a message. The Germans made the job difficult by changing keys as often as three times a day. Yet Turing and Knox, by applying advanced methods of statistical analysis, were able to shorten radically the time needed by code breakers to puzzle out the keys to rotor settings. As a result, the master cryptanalysts at Bletchley Park often were able to decipher messages just hours after they had been sent. Midway through the war, the British began to intercept messages ciphered according to another system, which they code-named Fish. The Germans called it *Schlüsselzusatz*—coding attachment—and used it to circulate information and orders among the highest levels of command, including that of Hitler himself. The *Schlüsselzusatz,* with a complement of 12 rotors, was a far

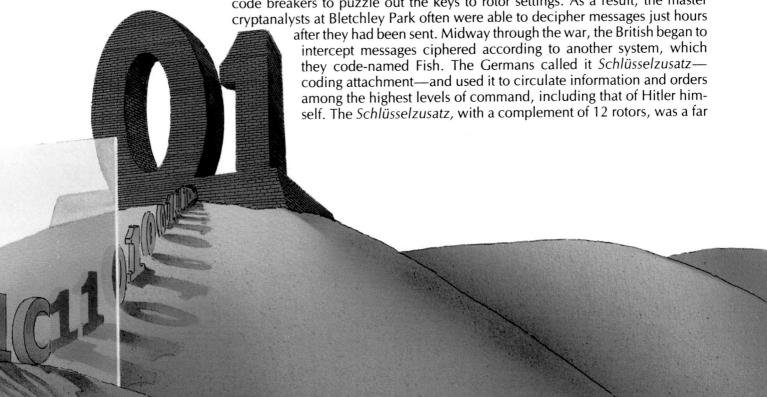

more complex machine than even late-model Enigmas, which could have as many as five rotors, and the new device produced ciphers that were correspondingly more difficult to penetrate.

The electromechanical devices at Bletchley Park, working with the speed of electric switches in a telephone exchange, operated much too slowly to break these improved ciphers. Responding to the new challenge in 1943, Turing prodded experimenters at the Post Office Research Station (the post office ran Britain's telephone systems) to build a faster, all-electronic code-breaking machine that would replace the plodding switches with lightning-fast vacuum tubes. Ultimately packed with 2,400 such tubes, this digital device predated the American ENIAC, the first large-scale computer, by two full years. Dubbed Colossus, the machine analyzed intercepted *Schlüsselzusatz* messages at the then-astonishing rate of 25,000 characters per second—fast enough to provide Allied battlefield commanders with timely foreknowledge of enemy intentions.

COMPUTER-AGE ENCRYPTION

By ushering in the age of electronic decryption techniques, Colossus marked a watershed in the history of cryptography. There could be only one defense against computers used to decipher messages: computers that could encipher them. Indeed, after the war, researchers began programming computers with encryption algorithms far more complex than those embodied in the rotors of an Enigma machine or a *Schlüsselzusatz*. The result was to increase the work factor to a level that more than matched the problem-solving potential of computers.

Like virtually all cryptography since Caesar's time, this new, computerized brand was kept under government wraps and employed almost exclusively to preserve military secrecy and guard diplomatic communications. But when time-sharing computer networks began to proliferate during the 1970s, they brought with them a widespread concern: that these networks, carriers of EFT messages and channels for proprietary information as well as confidential data about individuals, would be vulnerable to intruders and eavesdroppers. To foil them, mathematicians have formulated encryption schemes designed to protect electronic data in the private sector and in government agencies not charged with keeping official secrets.

Two encryption systems have led the way. One is a single-key system, in which data is both encrypted and decrypted with the same key, a sequence of eight numbers, each between zero and 127. The other is a two-key system; in this approach to cryptography, a pair of mathematically complementary keys, each containing as many as 200 digits, are used for encryption and decryption. In contrast with ciphers of earlier generations, where security depended in part on concealing the algorithm, confidentiality of a computer-encrypted message hinges solely on the secrecy of keys. Each system is thought to encrypt a message so inscrutably that the step-by-step mathematical algorithms can be made public without compromising security.

The single-key system, named the Data Encryption Standard (DES), was designated in 1977 as the official method for protecting unclassified computer data in agencies of the federal government. Its evolution began in 1973 when the U.S. National Bureau of Standards, responding to public concern about the confidentiality of computerized information outside military and diplomatic channels, invited the submission of data-encryption techniques as the first step toward an encryption scheme intended for public use.

The method selected by the bureau as the DES was developed by IBM researchers. During encryption, the DES algorithm divides a message into blocks of eight characters, then enciphers them one after another. Under control of the key, the letters and numbers of each block are scrambled no fewer than 16 times, resulting in eight characters of ciphertext *(pages 106-111)*.

AN INEXTRICABLE BOND

The DES links the enciphered blocks together in such a way that the encryption of each block, beginning with the second one, depends on the results of encoding the one that precedes it. Consequently, the final encrypted block is changed if a single character is altered anywhere in the message. This aspect of the DES is the basis for the Message Authentication Code, or MAC *(pages 110-111)*, which guarantees that any tampering with the contents of a message or with data filed away on disk or tape can be detected. The MAC can be used without encryption where the communications equipment in use cannot handle ciphertext and where it may be necessary to preserve the accuracy, though perhaps not the secrecy, of information passing between computers. For example, a bank may care little who finds out that it has transferred money from one account to another, but its reputation can be ruined if account numbers and transfer amounts are altered, whether accidentally or intentionally.

When cryptologists devise a new cipher such as the DES, others test it by trying to defeat it with two kinds of attack. One is known as the brute-force approach, an attempt to discover the key used to encrypt a message by systematically trying all possible keys. The other is an analytical attack, an effort to break the code by seeking out weaknesses in the algorithm that eliminate some of the possible keys from consideration.

Encompassing no fewer than 70 quadrillion possible keys, the DES appears secure against a brute-force attack. On average, an assailant would have to try half of them to find the one that unlocks the code. It has been estimated that this task would occupy even a speedy computer, able to generate one million trials per second, for 1,142 years. By then, the reason for making the attempt would have been long forgotten.

From an analytical standpoint, the DES appears equally sound. No cryptologist has found any alternative to trying all the keys one by one. Detractors point out that more than 200 of the DES's galaxy of keys are inferior ones. Called weak or semiweak or semi-semiweak keys by the experts, any of them might create clues in an encrypted message that could lead to its decipherment in less time than a brute-force attack would consume.

IBM and the Bureau of Standards—renamed the Institute of Standards and Technology in 1988—caution against employing the weak keys. But Carl Meyer, one of the developers of the DES, denies that most of them offer an advantage to an attacker. "It is debatable how weak is weak," he says. "I would not hesitate to use a semi-semiweak key. I personally do not think you can do anything with them." Critics also note that the DES algorithm could have employed a key of 16 numbers, twice the present length. Such a key, they point out, would have substantially increased the DES's work factor.

The Case for Encrypting Computer Transmissions

Confidential computer data, unless encrypted, is never more vulnerable to theft than during transmission from one computer to another. In most cases, such information travels via the telephone system. In the short time required for data to travel from sender to receiver, the system affords eavesdroppers numerous opportunities to intercept the information and sometimes to alter it.

The uncertain journey begins at a modem attached to the transmitting computer. Plugged into the modem is a telephone line identical to the one leading from any standard telephone. In an office building *(left, below)*, this line is routed behind walls and between ceilings and floors to a small room called a telephone closet.

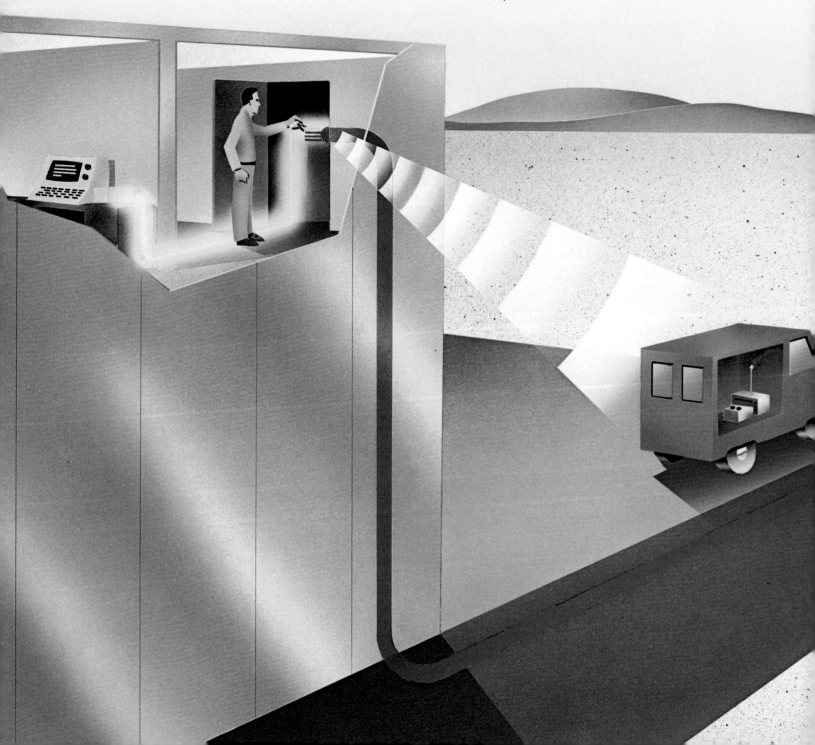

All the wires in a telephone closet are gathered into a cable, which is usually consolidated with others in the basement of the building. From there, a larger cable, about three inches in diameter, runs underground to a building called a central office, the headquarters for several exchanges (an exchange consists of local telephone numbers beginning with the same prefix). Here, data going to another computer on the exchange follows a similar path in reverse, directly to the receiving computer's modem. Information being transmitted to a modem on a different exchange is routed to the appropriate central office for connection. Between central offices, data may continue along its journey by cable, or it may be converted into a radio signal. Radio signals may be relayed to

their destination by so-called repeater stations on the ground or by communications satellites. Eavesdropping is simplest and least expensive at either end of the transmission, near the source of the data or near its destination. Once individual telephone lines have been merged into cables, they are difficult to identify. Isolating a particular signal from a satellite transmission is even more challenging and costly. But because an eavesdropper can listen in on a transmission from a distance, intercepting computer data from space carries little risk of discovery (page 96).

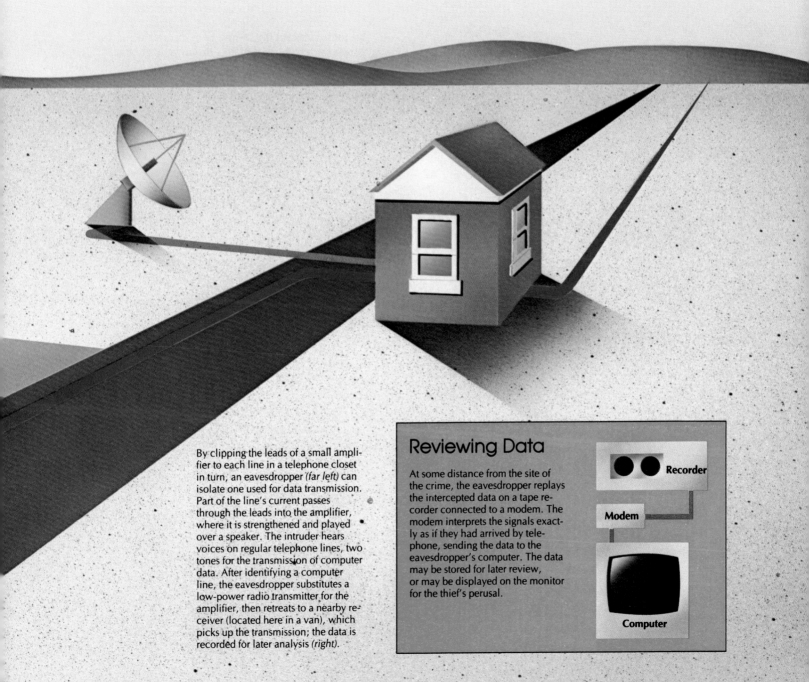

By clipping the leads of a small amplifier to each line in a telephone closet in turn, an eavesdropper (far left) can isolate one used for data transmission. Part of the line's current passes through the leads into the amplifier, where it is strengthened and played over a speaker. The intruder hears voices on regular telephone lines, two tones for the transmission of computer data. After identifying a computer line, the eavesdropper substitutes a low-power radio transmitter for the amplifier, then retreats to a nearby receiver (located here in a van), which picks up the transmission; the data is recorded for later analysis (right).

Reviewing Data

At some distance from the site of the crime, the eavesdropper replays the intercepted data on a tape recorder connected to a modem. The modem interprets the signals exactly as if they had arrived by telephone, sending the data to the eavesdropper's computer. The data may be stored for later review, or may be displayed on the monitor for the thief's perusal.

Recorder

Modem

Computer

Snatching Data
from the Ether

Computer data relayed to earth by a telephone-system communications satellite can be received from any location in an area covering millions of miles of the earth's surface. This broad coverage makes it quite easy for an eavesdropper to intercept computer data with a receiving system that employs an antenna similar to the satellite dishes commonly used with television sets.

Intercepting a communications satellite signal may be simple, but interpreting it is a daunting task. A satellite broadcasts on thousands of channels simultaneously, each representing one call, by means of an electronic process called multiplexing. The challenge for an eavesdropper is to discover which of the thousands of messages emanating from a satellite are of interest. Doing so demands an expert's knowledge of satellite communications as well as equipment costing several thousand dollars *(right)*.

Intercepting data from space is accomplished most easily if the eavesdropper's target leases a satellite communications channel. Without the certainty that the information always is transmitted over the same route, an eavesdropper must monitor all channels continuously. Generally, this constant surveillance would require resources comparable with those of a national government or a multinational corporation.

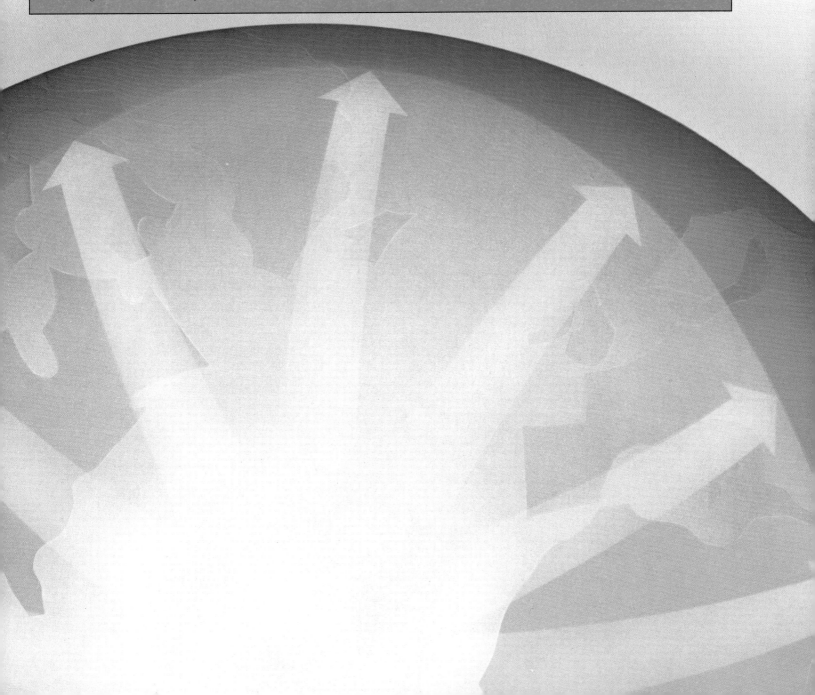

From Dish to Computer

A large antenna—the farther it is from the center of the reception area, the larger and more sensitive it must be —picks up the faint signals from a satellite and feeds them to a receiver. A device called a demultiplexer—shown here built into the receiver—is needed to separate the simultaneous channels transmitted by the satellite. After reviewing the incoming messages to discover which contains the sought-after computer data, the culprit records the information and—like the telephone-line eavesdropper on the preceding pages—plays the recorded data through a modem into a computer.

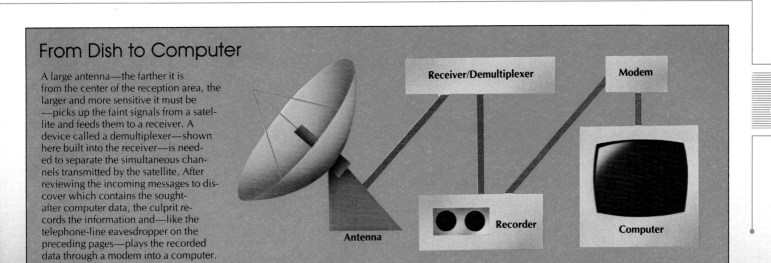

Receiver/Demultiplexer

Modem

Antenna

Recorder

Computer

Though usually confined to technical journals, the controversy over the Data Encryption Standard has from time to time spilled over into the popular press. What piqued the curiosity of the news media was the role played in the development of the DES by the supersecret National Security Agency. Created in 1952 to coordinate all code making and breaking related to national defense, the organization is so hush-hush that neighboring Washington bureaucrats joke that its initials, NSA, stand for "Never Say Anything" or "No Such Agency." Seeking to take advantage of the NSA's cryptological expertise, the researchers in charge of the program at the Bureau of Standards invited the agency's cipher brains to evaluate the DES algorithm to confirm that it was worthy of adoption. Critics likened huddling with the NSA in this manner, as one journalist wrote, to "putting the fox on sentry duty around the hen house."

Charges flew in the press that the NSA had insisted on limiting the length of the DES key to eight numbers instead of 16, purposely weakening the algorithm so that the agency could marshal its vast computer resources in a brute-force attack to break the cipher should the government see the need to do so. "The interesting thing," wrote David Kahn, a widely respected newspaperman and historian of cryptology, "is that while this cipher has been made just strong enough to withstand commercial attempts to break it, it has been left just weak enough to yield to government cryptanalysis."

Kahn and others have argued that only the NSA, or its counterpart in the government of another major nation, is likely to possess enough computer power to discover the key to a DES-encrypted message within a reasonable amount of time. Many cryptologists suspect that the agency has already accomplished this. To guard against the possibility that messages might be decoded, some users of the DES have modified the algorithm to accept a 16-number key. In any event, the U.S. Senate Select Committee on Intelligence investigated the NSA's involvement in the DES. And, although the committee found in 1979 that the agency did in fact persuade IBM to limit the key to eight numbers, the committee nonetheless came to the conclusion that the NSA "did not tamper with the design of the algorithm in any way."

BEYOND THE DES
As good as the DES is, obsolescence will almost certainly overtake it. The life span of encryption systems tends to be short; the older and more widely used a cipher is, the richer the potential payoff if it is cracked, and the greater the likelihood that someone has succeeded. A reasonable expectation is that the Data Encryption Standard will be superseded by new encryption algorithms, which in turn will give way to others.

Whatever single-key systems evolve will present a practical difficulty, common to all such ciphers, of protecting the secrecy of the key. The issue arises because the key must be in the hands of both sender and receiver. Getting it to them safely, especially when the key must be changed frequently to ensure communication security, has plagued code makers for centuries. And the task is further complicated by today's populous and far-flung computer networks. For example, to guarantee privacy of communication between any two subscribers in a network consisting of 1,000 members, 499,500 secret keys would be necessary, one for each possible combination of sender and receiver. Traditionally, keys have been distributed by a secure channel such as a trusted courier with an attaché case manacled to a wrist, a costly and time-consuming method. But with computers taking part in the encryption process, the time and effort required to exchange keys can be much reduced.

One technique of passing around keys employs a facility called a key-distribution center. Upon joining a network, subscribers confide their DES keys to the center, which is charged with keeping them secret. These keys are employed to encrypt not messages or data but additional DES keys, called session keys, as follows: When one subscriber wishes to communicate with another, the distribution center is asked for a session key different from any of the subscribers' keys. After randomly selecting such a key, the center encodes one copy with the sender's key and another copy with the recipient's, then transmits the session key to both parties. The sender, after decoding the session key, employs it to encrypt the message. The recipient, having also decoded the session key, uses it to read the message when it arrives.

Thus, only one key per terminal—the one on file at the distribution center—needs to be hand-delivered. Any other keys, because they are encrypted, can safely be passed electronically over the network. Furthermore, each message can have a different session key. If, by a phenomenal stroke of luck, the key were discovered, only the contents of a single communication would be compromised. Even if there is an unforeseen weakness in the algorithm, employing a different key for every transmission vastly complicates a code-breaker's job. Fresh keys so limit the amount of text encrypted with a particular key that even thorough analysis is unlikely to reveal a clue to the message.

THE TWO-KEY ALTERNATIVE

An entirely different approach to encryption, called the two-key, or public-key, system, simplifies the problem of key distribution and management. This approach to cryptography obviates the need for subscribers to share keys that must be kept confidential. In a public-key system, each subscriber has a pair of keys. One of them is the so-called public key, which is freely available to anyone who wishes to communicate with its owner. The other is a secret key, known only to its owner. Though either key can be used to encipher data or to decipher data encrypted with its mate, in most instances the public key is employed for encoding and the private key for decoding. Thus, anyone can send a secret message to anyone else by using the addressee's public key to encrypt the contents. But only the recipient of the message can make sense of it, since only that person has the private key.

This ingenious concept was first publicly proposed in 1976, at the peak of the controversy over the Data Encryption Standard. Indeed, Martin E. Hellman, the professor of electrical engineering at Stanford University who developed the public-key idea in collaboration with two of his students, Whitfield Diffie and Ralph Merkle, was also a leading critic of the National Security Agency's involvement with the DES.

Since then, however, the NSA has taken an interest in public-key cryptology, and Hellman has accepted research funding from the agency. "I wouldn't say I have been co-opted," Hellman replied when later asked about his view of the NSA. "But on the other hand, I am a lot more friendly."

The public-key concept developed by Merkle, Diffie and Hellman was based on a distinctive class of "secret-entrance" problems in mathematics known as trap doors. Like the openings left by systems programmers or unscrupulous hackers to bypass normal security procedures *(Chapter 3)*, these problems can be likened to a trap door cut into a theater stage. From below, it is easy to find the opening; a ladder or stairway marks the spot. But from above, the door blends with the stage floor in such a way that the door is difficult to detect. Similarly, mathematical trap doors are easy to solve in one direction, but working backward from the solution to the original problem is all but impossible. Merkle had first envisioned basing a public-key system on a trap-door problem while enrolled in an undergraduate computer course at the University of California at Berkeley, but his instructor there considered his approach impractical and a computer journal turned down his article on the subject.

Undiscouraged, Merkle sought out Hellman, and together they selected a classic trap-door problem to serve as the model for the cipher algorithm of their public-key system. Known among mathematicians as the trap-door knapsack, the problem is often described as that of determining how many cylinders—varying in length but identical in diameter—are contained, end to end, in a cylindrical knapsack of the same diameter. The strength of the algorithm derives from the fact that adding together a unique sequence of numbers is so simple a child can do it, but figuring out the original sequence, given only the sum, is a nearly hopeless task.

MATHEMATICAL RELATIONSHIPS

Employing advanced mathematical techniques, Hellman and Merkle devised complementary key-pairs, such that the only way to decipher a message encrypted with one member of the pair was to use the other member to unscramble the information. Encryption entailed assigning a number to each letter and then adding the numbers together. The decryption key recovered the numbers, from which the original text could be reconstructed. Though the keys are mathematically related, the nature of the kinship was believed to be such that a would-be code breaker could not figure out the private, decrypting key from a knowledge of the public, encrypting key. The code breaker's only recourse would be to mount an uneconomical brute-force attack in order to decipher a message by trial and error. Hellman confidently labeled the trap-door knapsack computationally secure.

Journalists hailed the system as unbreakable. "They've invented a practical code that can't be broken," asserted one magazine writer. "Once you've coded your information, no one—not the CIA, not the NSA, not even the IRS—can figure it out unless you have told them how." Merkle believed so strongly in the security of the algorithm that in 1976 he openly challenged cryptologists around the world to break it, offering a $100 reward—not much money, considering the effort required—to anyone who could do so.

In 1982, after years of analysis, Israeli mathematician Adi Shamir breached the trap-door-knapsack cipher while teaching at M.I.T. As evidence of his success, Shamir sent Merkle a seven-page abstract of his method together with a dog-eared copy of Merkle's old reward offer. In return he received a check for $100. Soon thereafter, Shamir's former colleague at M.I.T., mathematician Leonard

Adleman, of the University of Southern California, used Shamir's formula to break the knapsack cipher on a household-variety computer, an Apple II. "For all practical purposes," admitted Hellman's collaborator Whitfield Diffie, "trap-door knapsacks are flat on their back."

ENTER THE CHALLENGER

Shamir and Adleman had a personal stake in knocking the trap-door knapsack out of contention as a public-key encryption system. They are the authors, in collaboration with Ronald Rivest of M.I.T., of a competing version of the two-key system approach to cryptography. Designed in 1978, their version is known as the RSA system—for Rivest, Shamir, Adleman. In this cipher, the public and private keys are based on a trap door involving combinations of prime numbers. A number is prime if it can be evenly divided only by itself and the number one.

Multiplying one prime number by another yields a result, or product, that no other pair of prime numbers multiplied together can produce. A simple mathematical truism ices the cake: It is comparatively easy to confirm that a large number is prime but difficult to recover two such numbers after they have been multiplied together. This problem has proved more intractable than the knapsack scheme; it is no less time-consuming to solve by brute force and it is free of the mathematical chinks that doomed the knapsack cipher. For these reasons, the RSA system has fared better than Hellman, Merkle, and Diffie's attempt at a public-key cipher.

To maximize the security of the RSA system, its designers recommend the use of very large prime numbers to produce the public and private keys. For example, an RSA computer program selects at random two prime numbers that are each approximately 100 digits in length. The program then multiplies the two numbers together, and the resulting product—200 digits long—forms the basis for the two keys *(pages 112-113)*. A code breaker wanting to decipher an RSA-encrypted message thus would be faced with the millennia-long task of finding the prime factors—the original numbers multiplied together—of a 200-digit number. As far as anyone knows, the RSA system is computationally secure. Moreover, it is likely to remain so, barring unforeseen theoretical advances in the mathematics of factoring.

As with any public-key system, a confidential message normally is encrypted with the receiver's public key; it may then be decrypted only with the corresponding private key. In instances where the message itself need not be secret but the receiver must be certain of its authorship, the RSA system provides for a so-called digital signature *(pages 116-117)*. The sender's secret key is used to encrypt the message; the plaintext version may be transmitted along with the signature. At the receiving end, the signature is decoded with the sender's public key. If the result is gibberish, the receiver can be sure that the message did not come from its purported author.

When both secrecy of the message and verification of the sender's identity are important, the message may be double-encrypted, first with the sender's private key and then again with the receiver's public key. To decipher the transmission at the other end, the corresponding keys are applied in reverse order, first the receiver's secret key, then the sender's public key. With the integrity of the message and the certainty of the sender's identity thus ensured, a public-key encryption system can be used to consummate a legally binding contract electronically, and the parties need never meet face to face.

Actual use of RSA and other public-key techniques to encode large volumes of information has lagged behind that of the Data Encryption Standard. One reason is the DES's head start and its endorsement by the federal government. Another is that RSA has been implemented primarily in software, where it operates much more slowly than it would if it were built directly into a computer chip. For example, RSA encryption of just one block of text the length of its public key—about 80 characters—takes more than 100 times as long as DES encryption of a similar passage.

Nevertheless, RSA plays a valuable role in some DES-based systems as a way of solving the key-distribution problems of DES when used alone. In a typical arrangement, a sender encodes a message with DES, taking advantage of that algorithm's speed. Then the key used to code the message is itself encrypted by means of RSA. The scrambled DES key can then be safely transmitted with the message it encrypted.

The DES, too, has penetrated the marketplace less rapidly than security experts had anticipated. Not surprisingly, the leading customers are financial institutions, which encrypt bank-to-bank electronic transfers of funds as well as the personal identification numbers their patrons use at automatic teller machines. Lagging behind are such obvious areas of application as credit records and medical histories. One computer scientist, George Davida of the University of Wisconsin, has labeled these computerized data bases "electronic windows into the most intimate details of people's lives." In these areas, as Davida puts it, "encryption can serve as a curtain" to prevent others from looking in.

Some computer-security experts attribute the public's foot-dragging to the cost of encryption. Semiconductor companies mass-produce the DES algorithm by integrating the entire procedure into the circuitry of a single computer chip that is, in effect, an incredibly small cipher machine. Although DES microchips sell for about $15, the combination of hardware and software necessary to protect a single computer terminal can run as high as $1,500—more than the price of the terminal itself.

Other experts blame the same general apathy that has slowed the adoption of security measures intended to protect computers and their data from physical damage or destruction and from the ravages of teen-age hackers and computer-wielding thieves. As one security expert put it, "The managers of computing systems have not yet realized that information is a resource that is valuable and needs to be protected, just like money." Failing to provide security for sensitive information has much in common with the classic situation of smug homeowners who see no need for liability insurance until their dog bites a visitor.

A Pair of
Encryption
Alternatives

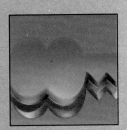

When banks, commodity brokers or shipping firms send information from one place to another by electronic means, they are increasingly likely to protect the confidentiality of the message by encryption. They may also encrypt data for storage on disk or tape to prevent a thief from being able to read private information. The workings of the two main systems—the Data Encryption Standard (DES) and a so-called public-key method—are explained on the following pages. The DES, developed by IBM and endorsed by the U.S. government for unclassified but sensitive applications, was established as a standard in 1977 (subject to periodic review). The public-key method was devised about the same time by scientists at Stanford University and M.I.T.

The two approaches have certain features in common. Both turn messages into gibberish by exploiting the number-manipulating prowess of computers. Both do the scrambling according to a set of steps—called an algorithm—that is public knowledge. And both achieve secrecy by the use of one-of-a-kind numbers called keys, which the algorithm uses to jumble the message in a unique way. The mathematical nature of the jumbling makes it virtually impossible—with present-day technology, anyway—to puzzle out the key unless the would-be code breaker is prepared to spend an impractical length of time in the attempt.

In certain respects, however, the two systems are very different. The DES requires the message sender and the receiver to share a single key, known only to the two of them. This raises the problem of key distribution: The secret key must itself be transmitted from sender to receiver (often by human courier), or must be agreed upon beforehand somehow, so that the message may be deciphered. In the public-key system, each user has a pair of keys—one that can be openly listed in the computer network's directory, and one that is known only to its possessor; the keys are mathematically linked in such a way that information encrypted by means of the receiver's public key can be deciphered only by the corresponding private key.

Tools of Concealment

Encryption and decryption are two sides of the same coin: A message is made unintelligible by altering it according to a certain procedure; it is made intelligible again by applying a reverse procedure. The jumbling can be done at the level of whole words (replacing the word "attack" with a specified word such as "blue," for example) or at the level of individual letters and numerals. Encryption systems that operate at the word level are technically known as codes; those that work at the character level are called cipher systems. Both the DES and the public-key method belong to the latter group. In the language of cryptography, the original message is known as the plaintext, the disguised message as the ciphertext. Either

the secret rules governing the method of encryption or the list of substitute words or letters (as in a code book, for instance) constitutes the key for encrypting and decrypting a message; sometimes both are required.

Five common techniques for scrambling a message are explained here; each encrypts the same message: SELL 100 SHARES OF ABCD INDUSTRIES. JOHN SMITH. As seen on the following pages, these treatments—substitution, blocking, permutation, expansion and compaction—are actually used repeatedly and in combination with one another during the ciphering of a message by the DES. (Throughout these examples, a dot symbol represents a space.)

SUBSTITUTION

The first step in this process is to create a substitution table (right), designating the replacement character for each character (including spaces and punctuation marks) that might appear in the message. Here, J is specified as the substitute for any A in the message, 2 for any F, and so on. The next line shows the ciphertext formed when the table is applied to the plaintext—SELL 100 SHARES OF ABCD INDUSTRIES. JOHN SMITH.—turning the first letter, S, into the numeral 5, for example. Below the ciphertext is the key, the reverse of the substitution table. Here, the substitute characters appear in conventional alphabetic and numeric order. Applying the table reveals the plaintext.

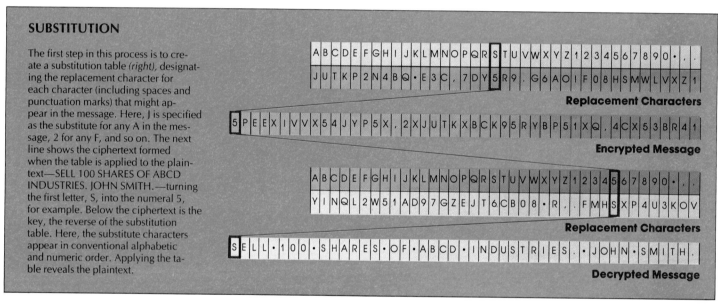

BLOCKING

Encryption systems often divide a message into blocks of characters that are independently manipulated. In the example here, the message was blocked into groups of eight characters and symbols (including a dot for each space). The resulting six blocks were then realigned vertically, with an extra space inserted into the sixth vertical block to make it even with the others. The ciphertext is created by blocking the new stack horizontally—to yield eight groups of six characters each—and transmitting these blocks in sequence. The receiver will group the ciphertext into blocks of six characters, stack them and read the message in the vertical columns.

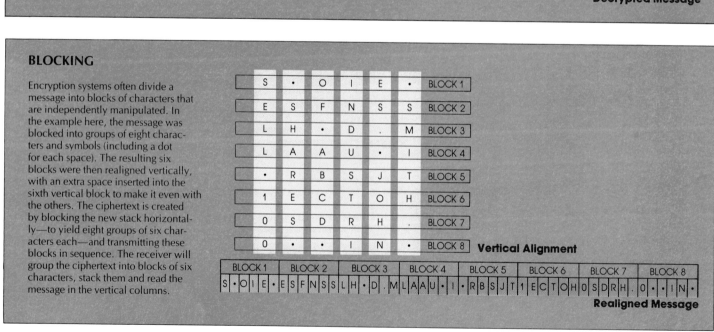

PERMUTATION

One of the most important encryption techniques is permutation, also called transposition. It involves moving characters around according to specific rules; the characters keep their identity but not their position—the opposite of substitution, in which characters keep their position but change their identity. In the example at right, the first step is to block the message into groups of eight. Then, in each group, the first and last characters are transposed, as are the middle two characters. The receiver subjects the ciphertext to exactly the same treatment in order to read the message.

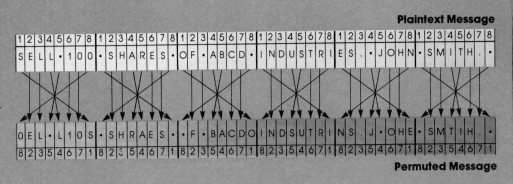

Plaintext Message

Permuted Message

EXPANSION

A simple way to obscure a message is to stretch it according to a fixed recipe. Here, the expansion follows the rules of the children's coding system called Pig Latin. Each word is altered by putting the first consonant sound last and adding the suffix "ay," as in "oybay" for "boy." (If a word begins with a vowel, the suffix "way" is

Plaintext Message

Expanded Message

simply added.) In actual cryptographic practice, the recipe would be much more elaborate. Moreover, expansion is often combined with other encryption techniques, since a cipher based on stretching alone is easily broken.

COMPACTION

Reducing the length of a message or the number of its blocks is another way of rendering the message unreadable. The formula for compaction in the elementary example shown here is to remove every third character, punctuation mark or space. The components that have been removed are transmitted separately to the message receiver (*bottom row*). That person knows the rule used for removal of the components and therefore knows where to reinsert them so that the message can be restored to its original form. The combination of the removed letters and the rule for removing them makes up the key for decrypting the message.

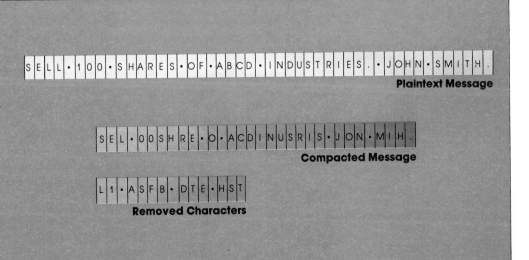

Plaintext Message

Compacted Message

Removed Characters

SEND MESSAGE, ENCRYPT WITH DATA
ENCRYPTION STANDARD

ENTER YOUR KEY

81 56 3 33 127 72 125 94

TO:

JULIA EDWARDS

TEXT:

SELL 100 SHARES OF ABCD INDUSTRIES.
JOHN SMITH.

In this example of transmitting a message by
the DES, the sender types an initial instruction
to select the method of encryption, then re-
sponds to prompts by the computer.

An Overview of the DES

As suggested by the pair of monitor screens on these pages,
computers do virtually all of the work in encrypted communications. The sender and receiver of a message never have to
see it in its ciphered form. When using the DES, for example,
the sender merely activates the program, then enters the secret key and the message; to read the message, the receiver
activates the same program and enters the same key. The
message appears on the screen with no indication of the
millions of arithmetical operations that sealed the information from prying eyes.

Encryption by the DES is usually done using a microchip
and other hardware specially designed for the job. The sophisticated multistep routine, or algorithm, built into the chip
includes the encryption tactics of substitution, blocking, per-

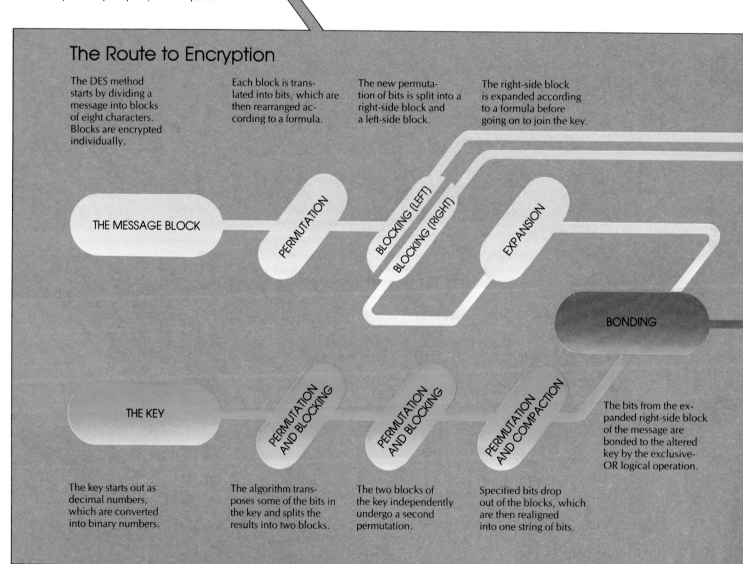

The Route to Encryption

The DES method
starts by dividing a
message into blocks
of eight characters.
Blocks are encrypted
individually.

Each block is trans-
lated into bits, which are
then rearranged ac-
cording to a formula.

The new permuta-
tion of bits is split into a
right-side block and
a left-side block.

The right-side block
is expanded according
to a formula before
going on to join the key.

THE MESSAGE BLOCK

PERMUTATION

BLOCKING (LEFT)

BLOCKING (RIGHT)

EXPANSION

BONDING

THE KEY

PERMUTATION
AND BLOCKING

PERMUTATION
AND BLOCKING

PERMUTATION
AND COMPACTION

The bits from the ex-
panded right-side block
of the message are
bonded to the altered
key by the exclusive-
OR logical operation.

The key starts out as
decimal numbers,
which are converted
into binary numbers.

The algorithm trans-
poses some of the bits in
the key and splits the
results into two blocks.

The two blocks of
the key independently
undergo a second
permutation.

Specified bits drop
out of the blocks, which
are then realigned
into one string of bits.

mutation, expansion and compaction. An additional procedure—a logical operation called exclusive-OR *(box, below)*—is used to bond components of the cipher at various points along the way. Although the algorithm is fixed, a given message or piece of data can be encrypted in 70 quadrillion different ways—the number of possible secret keys the system will allow. Clearly, then, key management—the ensuring of key secrecy—is a principal factor in guaranteeing the security of the message or data.

Below is a flow chart of the basic process (a more detailed explanation appears on pages 108-111). The first step in the encryption chain is to divide the message into blocks. Each block is then individually subjected to the steps indicated in the chart. But that is just the beginning: Before the block is completely encrypted, it must cycle through 15 additional rounds of the process; each round will impose the same sequence of steps shown in the chart.

CHECK MESSAGES

JOHN SMITH OCTOBER 25 10:10 AM

READ MESSAGE, DECRYPT WITH DATA
ENCRYPTION STANDARD

ENTER YOUR KEY

81 56 3 33 127 72 125 94

SELL 100 SHARES OF ABCD INDUSTRIES.
JOHN SMITH. 8V•?

The receiver checks her electronic mail and engages in a dialogue with the computer to read the message. The last three characters and a space verify an accurate transmission.

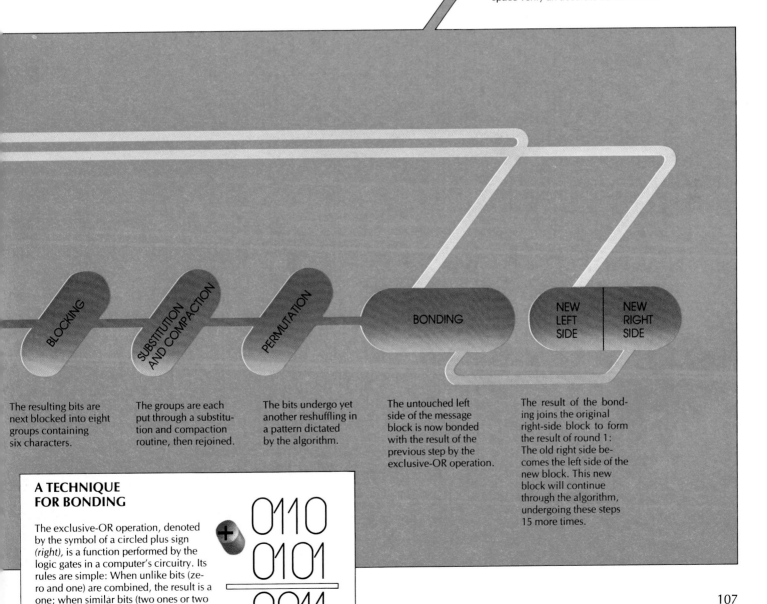

BLOCKING

SUBSTITUTION AND COMPACTION

PERMUTATION

BONDING

NEW LEFT SIDE

NEW RIGHT SIDE

The resulting bits are next blocked into eight groups containing six characters.

The groups are each put through a substitution and compaction routine, then rejoined.

The bits undergo yet another reshuffling in a pattern dictated by the algorithm.

The untouched left side of the message block is now bonded with the result of the previous step by the exclusive-OR operation.

The result of the bonding joins the original right-side block to form the result of round 1: The old right side becomes the left side of the new block. This new block will continue through the algorithm, undergoing these steps 15 more times.

A TECHNIQUE FOR BONDING

The exclusive-OR operation, denoted by the symbol of a circled plus sign *(right)*, is a function performed by the logic gates in a computer's circuitry. Its rules are simple: When unlike bits (zero and one) are combined, the result is a one; when similar bits (two ones or two zeros) are combined, the result is a zero.

$$\oplus \quad \frac{0110}{0101}$$
$$\overline{0011}$$

107

A Close-Up of the DES

All of the jumbling wrought by the DES algorithm takes place in the computer's language of bits—the binary digits zero and one. The key and the message are translated into binary by different means. Initially, the key is made up of eight decimal numbers; these are simply turned into their seven-bit binary equivalents, with an extra bit added at the end for checking. The DES algorithm uses only the first seven bits for encryption, however; the checking bit is ignored. Thus, when put into action by the DES, a key is eight decimal numbers times seven bits, or 56 bits long.

The message is converted to binary by expressing it in ASCII—the American Standard Code for Information Interchange. ASCII, shown in abbreviated form on pages 120-121, is an agreed-upon list of binary representations of the roman alphabet, the numbers of the decimal system, punctuation marks and other keyboard symbols. ASCII codes are eight bits in length—seven plus a leading checking bit. Because the message is encrypted in blocks of eight characters, each block starts out as 64 bits *(opposite, top).*

Provided the key remains secret, its 56-bit length is a formidable defense against an attack on the ciphertext. A would-be code breaker using a computer to test all possible combinations of 56 zeros and ones at the rate of one million tests a second could expect to take 1,142 years to complete the task.

An additional safeguard is the sheer complexity of the algorithm. As indicated by the flow chart on the preceding pages, the 64 bits of each block of the message are permuted and divided into two sides that proceed separately through the algorithm to form the starting point for the next round of encryption. Each block must pass through 16 rounds of garbling, with the key jumbled into a new form, or subkey, for each round. Each subkey is derived from the one preceding it, and each is bonded with a piece of the message by the exclusive-OR operation, so that the message is thoroughly imbued with the key's uniqueness.

A detailed example of the DES in action is traced on these two pages. Under the control of a randomly generated key *(below),* the first of the 16 rounds of ciphering is done on the initial eight-unit block of the message SELL 100 SHARES OF ABCD INDUSTRIES. JOHN SMITH.

The Creation of Keys

The key shared by sender and receiver consists of eight decimal numbers, each between 0 and 127. Typically, a key is generated by computer to ensure that the numbers are random—lacking a detectable pattern. In this example, the numbers making up the key are 81, 56, 3, 33, 127, 72, 125 and 94. The computer converts them to their binary equivalents, with leading zeros to fill out the seven digits required by the algorithm and an eighth bit for checking. The bits are then grouped into blocks, the checking bit is ignored, and the bits are subjected to permutation and compaction. The process is repeated 15 times to produce unique subkeys for each subsequent round.

Each bit in the binary equivalent for each decimal number *(top)* is given a position number *(bottom).*

The bits are resequenced (old position numbers are on top), and two 28-digit blocks are formed.

In each block, bits are shifted one place to the left (the first goes to the end). In subsequent rounds, the bits may shift more places.

Bits are dropped and the 48-bit result is subkey 1. New subkeys are made by going back a step, doing another left shift and repeating this step.

A Message Block's Progress

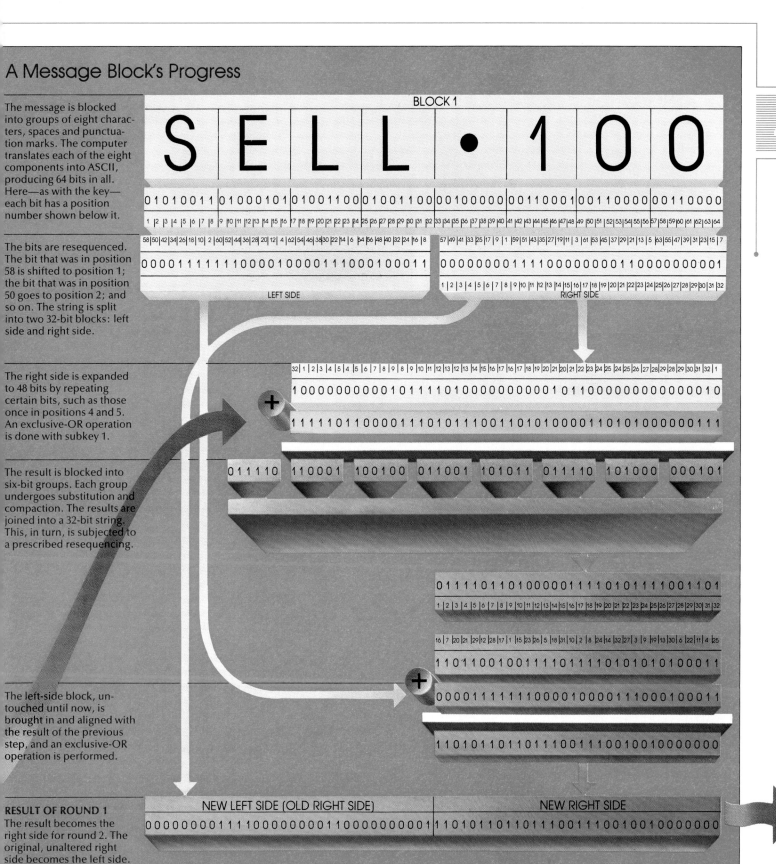

The message is blocked into groups of eight characters, spaces and punctuation marks. The computer translates each of the eight components into ASCII, producing 64 bits in all. Here—as with the key—each bit has a position number shown below it.

The bits are resequenced. The bit that was in position 58 is shifted to position 1; the bit that was in position 50 goes to position 2; and so on. The string is split into two 32-bit blocks: left side and right side.

The right side is expanded to 48 bits by repeating certain bits, such as those once in positions 4 and 5. An exclusive-OR operation is done with subkey 1.

The result is blocked into six-bit groups. Each group undergoes substitution and compaction. The results are joined into a 32-bit string. This, in turn, is subjected to a prescribed resequencing.

The left-side block, untouched until now, is brought in and aligned with the result of the previous step, and an exclusive-OR operation is performed.

RESULT OF ROUND 1
The result becomes the right side for round 2. The original, unaltered right side becomes the left side.

BLOCK 1

S E L L · 1 0 0

0101001101000101010011000100110000100000001100010011000000110000
1 2 3 4 5 6 7 8 9 10 11 12 13 14 15 16 17 18 19 20 21 22 23 24 25 26 27 28 29 30 31 32 33 34 35 36 37 38 39 40 41 42 43 44 45 46 47 48 49 50 51 52 53 54 55 56 57 58 59 60 61 62 63 64

58 50 42 34 26 18 10 2 60 52 44 36 28 20 12 4 62 54 46 38 30 22 14 6 64 56 48 40 32 24 16 8 | 57 49 41 33 25 17 9 1 59 51 43 35 27 19 11 3 61 53 45 37 29 21 13 5 63 55 47 39 31 23 15 7

00001111111000010000111000100011 | 00000000111100000001100000000001

LEFT SIDE | RIGHT SIDE
1 2 3 4 5 6 7 8 9 10 11 12 13 14 15 16 17 18 19 20 21 22 23 24 25 26 27 28 29 30 31 32

32 1 2 3 4 5 4 5 6 7 8 9 8 9 10 11 12 13 12 13 14 15 16 17 16 17 18 19 20 21 20 21 22 23 24 25 24 25 26 27 28 29 28 29 30 31 32 1

100000000001011110100000000001011000000000000010
111101100001101110011010100011010100000011 1

+

011110 110001 100100 011001 101011 011110 101000 000101

01111011010000011110101110011101
1 2 3 4 5 6 7 8 9 10 11 12 13 14 15 16 17 18 19 20 21 22 23 24 25 26 27 28 29 30 31 32

16 7 20 21 29 12 28 17 1 15 23 26 5 18 31 10 2 8 24 14 32 27 3 9 19 13 30 6 22 11 4 25

11011001011110111010101010100011

00001111111000010000111000100011

+

11010110110111001110010010000000

NEW LEFT SIDE (OLD RIGHT SIDE) | NEW RIGHT SIDE

00000000111100000001100000000001 | 11010110110111001110010010000000

109

A Round-by-Round, Block-by-Block Linkage

At the end of round 1, the first block of the message has scarcely begun its ordeal; 15 more rounds are required before the DES algorithm moves on to encrypt the next block. For each message block, the same subkeys are used at identical stages of encryption—subkey 1 for round 1, subkey 2 for round 2 and so on.

The cipher for the first message block is shown as a ciphertext translation of the computer's 64-bit result; these bits will be bonded to the next block by an exclusive-OR operation. Not all of the enciphered results are printable; they appear as blanks (shown here as dot symbols), but the computer keeps track of their ciphered meaning.

A block-linking stratagem adds to the defensive strength of the encrypted message: The cipher of each message block is bonded to the next block by an exclusive-OR operation, so that every step of the encryption process shapes every subsequent step. The last block of an encrypted message (or a portion of the block) can thus act as a Message Authentication Code (MAC). Sent separately from the ciphered message, the MAC is used to check the accuracy of the transmission: The receiver reencrypts the message; if the encrypted last block differs from the MAC, it means the message was altered en route. (A sender may also append a MAC to the end of a plaintext message as a check against alteration.)

The first 32 bits—four units—of the last block are often picked as the MAC. The receiver recomputes the message and looks for a match.

The Power of Two Keys

SEND MESSAGE, ENCRYPT WITH PUBLIC KEY

TO:

JULIA EDWARDS

TEXT:

SELL 100 SHARES OF ABCD INDUSTRIES. JOHN SMITH.

For all its virtues, the Data Encryption Standard has its flaws. To begin with, ensuring the secure distribution of secret keys between each pair of senders and receivers is difficult, especially when the network of users is large. A 1,000-person network, for example, would require almost half a million keys to guarantee the privacy of each pair. More important, the MAC feature, though it acts as a check on the information transmitted, does not prevent a person from sending himself a message (to order a transfer of funds, for instance).

The public-key system of encryption addresses both of these problems. For a network of 1,000 persons only 2,000 keys are needed. Each user has a pair of mathematically related keys: One is public knowledge within the network, the other is known only to its owner. The sender encrypts a message using the receiver's public key; the receiver decrypts it with the mathematically related private key. The sender's keys come into play to create and then to decrypt a

In this example, as with the DES, users of the public-key system respond to a series of computer prompts and observe none of the ciphering process. Here, sender John Smith activates the program and identifies the addressee, Julia Edwards. Behind the scenes, the computer retrieves Julia Edwards' public key and employs it to encrypt John Smith's message.

ASSIGNING NUMERIC VALUES

ENCRYPTION

Converting a Message to Numbers

PRESCRIBED NUMERIC VALUES

A	B	C	D	E	F	G	H	I	J	K	L	M	N	O	P	Q	R	S	T	U	V	W	X	Y	Z	0	1	2	3	4	5	6	7	8	9	•	,	.
1	2	3	4	5	6	7	8	9	10	11	12	13	14	15	16	17	18	19	20	21	22	23	24	25	26	27	28	29	30	31	32	33	34	35	36	37	38	39

CONVERTING THE MESSAGE

S	E	L	L	•	1	0	0	•	S	H	A	R	E	S	•	O	F	•	A	B	C	D	•	I	N	D	U	S	T	R	I	E	S	•	J	O	H	N	•	S	M	I	T	H	.
19	5	12	12	37	28	27	27	37	19	8	1	18	5	19	37	15	6	37	1	2	3	4	37	9	14	4	21	19	20	18	9	5	19	37	10	15	8	14	37	19	13	9	20	8	39

Before a message can be encrypted by the public-key method, it must be blocked and each block assigned a numerical value. Blocks may vary in size, from one character to several; and numerical values may be assigned in many ways, within constraints imposed by the system. In the example used here, each character is treated as a block, and a simple number-assigning system is used: A = 1, B = 2, C = 3, D = 4, and so on (table at top).

When John Smith types the message into his computer, every character, space and punctuation mark is assigned its specified numerical value (table, above). These numbers will be individually subjected to a series of arithmetical operations controlled by both the public key and the private key.

N = 1377077135085831792882099980596806736143857987956799828060398899205926178656291079517890977230143376854226347735425165905206600143 2

special signature that is used to verify the source of the message *(pages 116-117).*

The strength of the public-key system depends on the nature of the relationship between the public and private keys; given a public key, it is virtually impossible to derive the private one. The system described here and on the following pages—designed by Ronald Rivest, Adi Shamir and Leonard Adleman while at M.I.T.—creates the keys by first multiplying two prime numbers (numbers evenly divisible only by themselves and one). Figuring out the primes from the product of the multiplication—a process called factoring—is exceedingly difficult. Small numbers are used here for clarity, but the algorithm actually works with very large numbers; on the bottom of these pages, for instance, is a 203-digit product of two primes. Factoring such a number would be the first step in trying to break a key; with present methods, it would take a computer millions of years.

CHECK MESSAGES

JOHN SMITH OCTOBER 25 10:10 AM

READ MESSAGE, DECRYPT WITH PUBLIC KEY

ENTER KEY FILE NAME

JEFILE

SELL 100 SHARES OF ABCD INDUSTRIES. JOHN SMITH.

AND DECRYPTION

SIGNING AND SEALING

On the receiving end, Julia Edwards periodically checks her computer for messages. When the computer indicates that one has arrived, she specifies that it be decrypted by the public-key method. She enters the name of the protected computer file that contains her private key: Jefile. Decryption proceeds invisibly, and the message then appears on the screen.

Creating Julia Edwards' Keys

1. Each user has a public and a private key, and each key has two parts. To create Julia Edwards' keys, two prime numbers, customarily designated P and Q, are generated by an operator at a central computer. (To qualify, a prime number must pass a special mathematical test.) Here, P is 7, Q is 17.

2. In this simplified example, the two primes are multiplied, and the result—N—will be the first part of both keys. Here, N is 119.

3. Next, an odd number is chosen, in this case, 5. (This number—designated E—must also pass a special mathematical test.) It forms the second part of the public key.

4. To create the second part of the private key, the numbers are multiplied: P minus 1 (6, in this case) times Q minus 1 (16) times E minus 1 (4). The result is 384.

5. Next, 1 is added to the result of the previous step, yielding 385.

6. The sum is divided by E (5). The result of the division, 77 (designated D), is the second part of Julia Edwards' private key.

$$1 \quad P = 7, \ Q = 17$$

$$2 \quad 7 \times 17 = 119 = N$$

$$3 \quad E = 5$$

$$4 \quad 6 \times 16 \times 4 = 384$$

$$5 \quad 384 + 1 = 385$$

$$6 \quad 385 \div 5 = 77 = D$$

PUBLIC KEY

119 5

PRIVATE KEY

119 77

At the end of the procedure Julia Edwards has a public key (119 5) and a private key (119 77). In reality, these numbers would be many digits long; as indicated on the screen above, she would keep the private key in a protected computer file.

The Public-Key System in Action

Once a message has been committed to public-key encryption, it is virtually beyond retrieval. Even if the sender wanted to pry apart the ciphertext for some reason, it would be a hopeless task. The cipher can be unscrambled only by the person who possesses the private key corresponding to the public key that was used for encrypting the message—that is, the addressee. Thus, any user with access to the network's directory of public keys may send anyone else a confidential

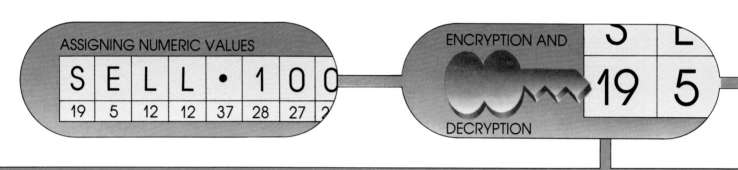

ASSIGNING NUMERIC VALUES

S	E	L	L	•	1	0	0
19	5	12	12	37	28	27	2

ENCRYPTION AND DECRYPTION

S	L
19	5

The Arithmetic of Locking and Unlocking

The number 19, assigned to the letter S, is raised to the fifth power (multiplied by itself five times), as dictated by the second part of Julia Edwards' public key (5).

The result of 19 raised to the fifth power—2,476,099—is divided by the first part of Julia Edwards' public key, the number 119.

The division yields the number 20,807 and a remainder of 66. Only the remainder is important: It is the value of the encrypted letter S.

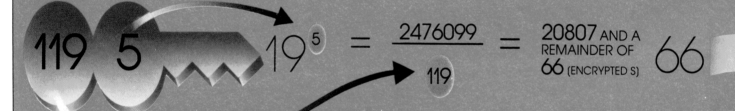

$$119 \quad 5 \qquad 19^5 = \frac{2476099}{119} = 20807 \text{ AND A REMAINDER OF } 66 \text{ (ENCRYPTED S)} \quad 66$$

$$119 \quad 5 \qquad 5^5 = \frac{3125}{119} = 26 \text{ AND A REMAINDER OF } 31 \text{ (ENCRYPTED E)} \quad 31$$

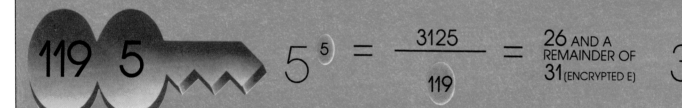

The next letter of the message, E, has the assigned value 5. Using the second part of the public key, this number is raised to the fifth power.

The result of multiplying 5 by itself five times—3,125—is divided by the other part of the public key, 119.

The division yields the number 26 and a remainder of 31. Again, only the remainder is significant. It is the value of the encrypted letter E.

message; but only the intended recipient can decipher it.

The process of ciphering and deciphering is shown below, using the artificially small numbers that make up Julia Edwards' keys and working on the first two letters of the message SELL 100 SHARES OF ABCD INDUSTRIES. JOHN SMITH. Unlike the DES—which manipulates the bits assigned to each component of the message through such techniques as substitution and compaction—the public-key system em-

ploys a purely mathematical process. In order to encrypt the message, the two numbers that make up the receiver's public key are used to perform computations on the numerical value assigned to every character, space and punctuation mark. Because the numbers in the public key have an inverse relationship with the numbers in the private key, the message may be decrypted by performing similar computations with the private-key numbers.

SIGNING AND SEALING

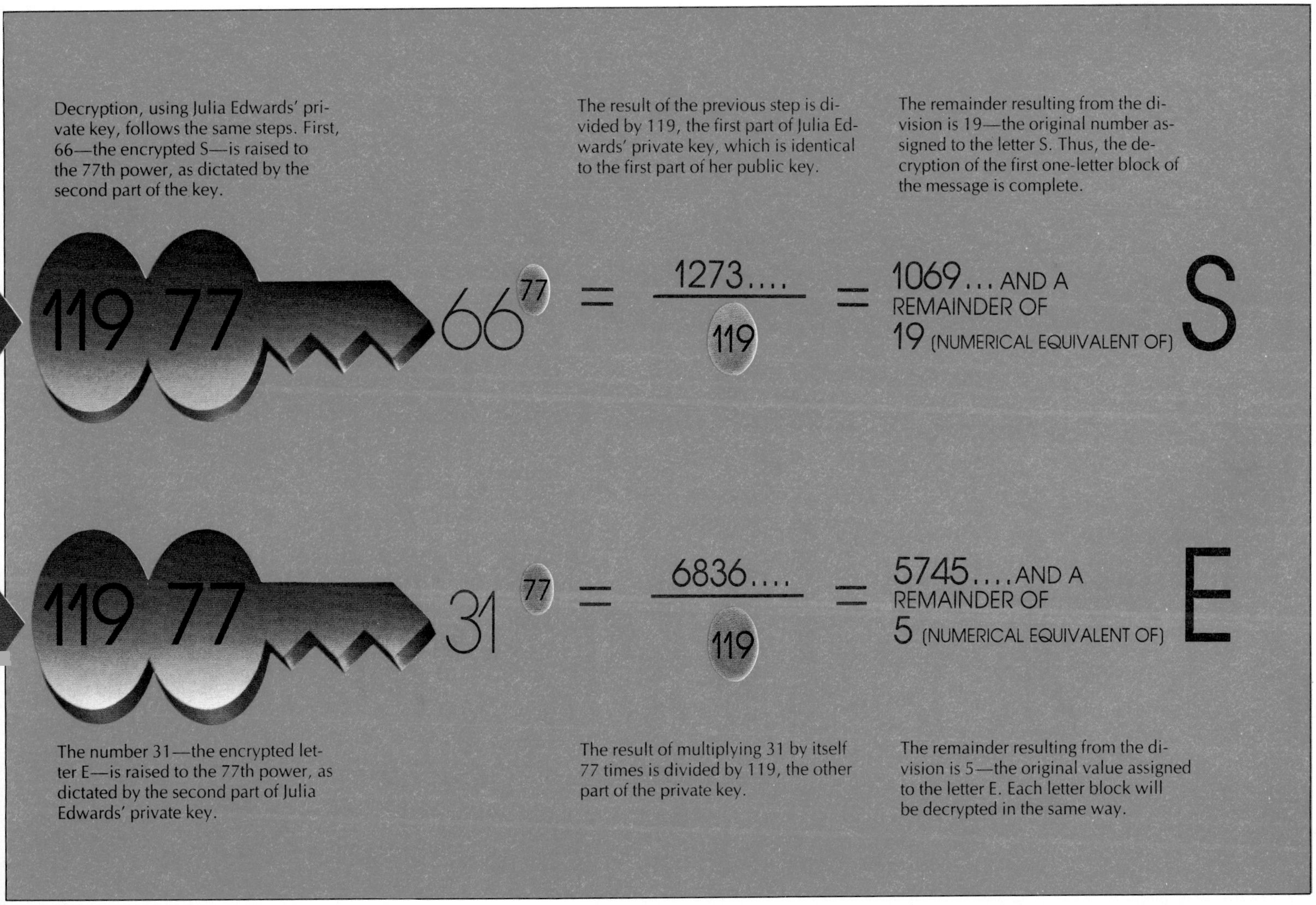

Decryption, using Julia Edwards' private key, follows the same steps. First, 66—the encrypted S—is raised to the 77th power, as dictated by the second part of the key.

The result of the previous step is divided by 119, the first part of Julia Edwards' private key, which is identical to the first part of her public key.

The remainder resulting from the division is 19—the original number assigned to the letter S. Thus, the decryption of the first one-letter block of the message is complete.

$$119 \quad 77 \qquad 66^{77} = \frac{1273....}{119} = 1069... \text{ AND A REMAINDER OF } 19 \text{ (NUMERICAL EQUIVALENT OF) } S$$

$$119 \quad 77 \qquad 31^{77} = \frac{6836....}{119} = 5745.... \text{ AND A REMAINDER OF } 5 \text{ (NUMERICAL EQUIVALENT OF) } E$$

The number 31—the encrypted letter E—is raised to the 77th power, as dictated by the second part of Julia Edwards' private key.

The result of multiplying 31 by itself 77 times is divided by 119, the other part of the private key.

The remainder resulting from the division is 5—the original value assigned to the letter E. Each letter block will be decrypted in the same way.

A Twice-Scrambled Certificate of Origin

One of the chief attributes of the public-key system is its ability to verify the identity of the source of a message. This is made possible by a simple variation on the encryption techniques described on the preceding pages. Precisely how it is done depends on whether or not secrecy is important.

If the contents of a message are not secret but the receiver must be certain of the sender's identity, the message may be signed—that is, transmitted as a so-called digital signature. A signature is exceedingly difficult to counterfeit, because the message is encrypted not with the receiver's public key but

ENCRYPTION AND DECRYPTION

SIGNING AND SEALING

S	E
19	5

Two Tiers of Decryption

To begin the encryption technique called signing, the value of the letter S (19)—is raised to the 27th power, as dictated by the second part of John Smith's private key.

The result of raising 19 to the 27th power is divided by 55, the first part of his private key.

The division yields a very large number, which is disregarded, and a remainder of 24. This completes the signing process for the letter S; only John Smith's public key can decrypt it.

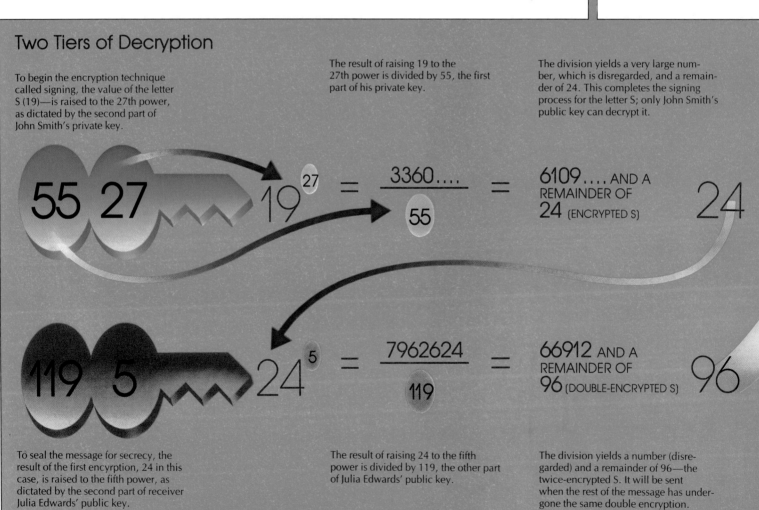

$$55 \quad 27 \qquad 19^{27} = \frac{3360\ldots.}{55} = 6109\ldots. \text{ AND A REMAINDER OF } 24 \text{ (ENCRYPTED S)} \qquad 24$$

$$119 \quad 5 \qquad 24^{5} = \frac{7962624}{119} = 66912 \text{ AND A REMAINDER OF } 96 \text{ (DOUBLE-ENCRYPTED S)} \qquad 96$$

To seal the message for secrecy, the result of the first encyrption, 24 in this case, is raised to the fifth power, as dictated by the second part of receiver Julia Edwards' public key.

The result of raising 24 to the fifth power is divided by 119, the other part of Julia Edwards' public key.

The division yields a number (disregarded) and a remainder of 96—the twice-encrypted S. It will be sent when the rest of the message has undergone the same double encryption.

with the sender's private key. Anyone who knew that the incoming message was sent by John Smith, for example, could decrypt it using John Smith's public key. But a forgery—a message encrypted with a different private key and transmitted as coming from John Smith—would produce only gibberish when the real John Smith's public key was applied to decrypt it. (A nonsecret message could also be transmitted as plaintext, with the encrypted signature appended to it in order to verify the source.)

When secrecy as well as verification is a matter of importance, the message may in effect be sealed by adding a layer of encryption to the signed message, as shown below. After encrypting the message with his private key (signing it), John Smith applies the receiver's—in this instance, Julia Edwards'—public key to the ciphertext, sealing it from any eyes but hers. To render the message intelligible, Julia Edwards

must go through a similar two-step procedure. First she must decrypt the transmission with her private key, to undo the seal; then she has to apply John Smith's public key, revealing the message and, in the process, verifying that the message was indeed transmitted by John Smith.

Despite its strength as a cipher and its antiforgery feature, the public-key system demands a certain amount of vigilance on the part of its users. Although public keys could theoretically be broadcast to all the world, they are normally made available only to the members of the network in which they are used; this prevents an outsider from even attempting forgery. Access to public keys can be restricted by keeping them in a protected directory or in a protected computer file (pages 73-85). Private keys, of course, must be protected with even more stringent precautions, else both secrecy and verification are nullified.

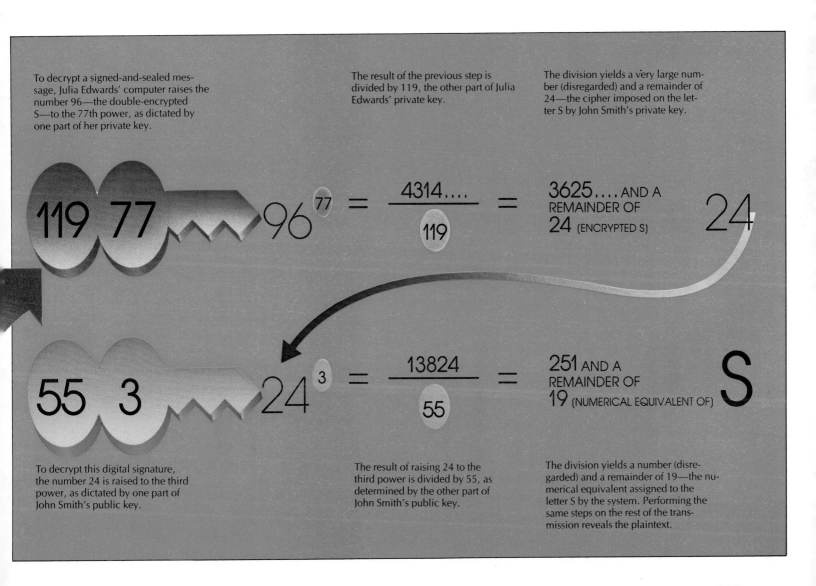

To decrypt a signed-and-sealed message, Julia Edwards' computer raises the number 96—the double-encrypted S—to the 77th power, as dictated by one part of her private key.

The result of the previous step is divided by 119, the other part of Julia Edwards' private key.

The division yields a very large number (disregarded) and a remainder of 24—the cipher imposed on the letter S by John Smith's private key.

$$119 \quad 77 \qquad 96^{77} = \frac{4314....}{119} = 3625....\text{ AND A REMAINDER OF } 24 \text{ (ENCRYPTED S)} \qquad 24$$

$$55 \quad 3 \qquad 24^{3} = \frac{13824}{55} = 251 \text{ AND A REMAINDER OF } 19 \text{ (NUMERICAL EQUIVALENT OF) } S$$

To decrypt this digital signature, the number 24 is raised to the third power, as dictated by one part of John Smith's public key.

The result of raising 24 to the third power is divided by 55, as determined by the other part of John Smith's public key.

The division yields a number (disregarded) and a remainder of 19—the numerical equivalent assigned to the letter S by the system. Performing the same steps on the rest of the transmission reveals the plaintext.

Glossary

Access control: the use of either physical safeguards such as locks or software safeguards such as passwords to prevent unauthorized access to a computer.

Access-control list: a list of users who are allowed access to a program or data file, including the extent of each user's authorized access; see read-access and write-access.

Algorithm: a step-by-step procedure for solving a problem; in encryption, the mathematical procedure used to create a cipher.

Amplifier: an electronic device that increases the voltage or power level of a signal.

Analog: the representation of changes in a continuous physical variable (sound, for example) by continuous changes in another physical variable (such as electrical current).

Analog-to-digital converter: a device that changes an analog signal into digital information.

Analytical attack: an attempt to break a code or cipher key by discovering flaws in its encryption algorithm; see also brute-force attack.

Assembly language: a low-level programming language, just above the zeros and ones of machine code, that employs short mnemonic codes to tell the computer to carry out operations.

Audit trail: a chronological record of computer activity automatically maintained to trace all use of the computer; for security purposes, it is preferable that the record be maintained by the operating system.

Authentication: the process of establishing the validity of a message or of verifying a user's authorization for access to data.

Backup facility: a guarded building whose climate-controlled vaults contain copies of data and software.

Bit: the smallest unit of information in a binary computer, represented by a single zero or one. The word "bit" is a contraction of "binary digit."

Black box: a homemade electronic device that stops the signal indicating a completed telephone call so that the call does not trigger billing machinery; see also phone phreaking.

Blue box: a homemade electronic device that synthesizes single-frequency telephone-dialing tones to defeat long-distance billing machinery.

Browsing: see scavenging.

Brute-force attack: a computerized trial-and-error attempt to decode a cipher by trying every possible key; also called exhaustive attack.

Cable: a group of insulated conductors encased in a protective sheath.

Callback routine: a method of controlling telephone access to a computer with a device that registers an authorized password, then hangs up and calls back to that user's authorized phone number.

Central office: local telephone-switching equipment for a given geographic area.

Channel: an electronic communications path within a computer system or in telecommunications between systems.

Checksum: results of mathematical computations involving the bits in a sector on a floppy disk; used to verify sector accuracy.

Cipher: an encryption system that arbitrarily represents each character by one or more other characters.

Ciphertext: the encrypted, unintelligible text produced by a cipher.

Circuit: a closed network through which current can flow.

Code: an encryption system whose components represent characters, words or sentences.

Cold site: a backup facility equipped with communications gear, computer cables and air conditioning, so that it is possible to install computers quickly in case of disaster at the primary site.

Computer network: a system of two or more computers connected by communications channels.

Cryptography: the enciphering and deciphering of messages using secret ciphers or codes.

Data diddling: unauthorized alteration of data as it is entered or stored in a computer.

Data Encryption Standard (DES): a single-key system endorsed by the National Institute of Standards and Technology (formerly the National Bureau of Standards) for encryption of commercial data.

Data leakage: the theft of data or software.

Decryption: using the right key to convert ciphertext to plaintext.

Degausser: a device whose strong magnetic field erases disks and tapes so that they can be reused or discarded.

Demultiplexer: a circuit that separates one input signal from multiple accompanying signals and distributes it to an output line; see also multiplexer.

Digital: pertaining to the representation, manipulation or transmission of information by discrete, or on-off, signals.

Digital signature: a verification method in public-key ciphers in which the message is encrypted with the sender's private key and the recipient decrypts the signature with the sender's public key.

Disaster-recovery plan (DRP): a prearranged procedure to quickly transfer backup programs and data to a backup computer in case of catastrophic damage to a primary computer.

Disk: a round magnetic plate—or a stack of such plates—usually made of plastic or metal, used for data storage.

Disk drive: the mechanism that rotates a storage disk and reads or records data.

Eavesdropping: unauthorized interception of data transmissions.

Electromagnetic emanations: data-bearing signals radiated through the air or through conductors.

Electromagnetic pulse (EMP): the surge of electromagnetic energy generated by a nuclear explosion, which can disable or destroy computers and other transistorized devices.

Electronic funds transfer (EFT): a computerized transaction, conducted via long-distance telephone lines, that instantly moves money between computer accounts.

Encryption: scrambling data or messages with a cipher or code so that they are unreadable without a secret key.

Exhaustive attack: see brute-force attack.

File: a collection of related information stored in a computer.

Frequency: the rate in cycles per second at which an electronic signal is repeated.

Hacker: a computer enthusiast; also, one who seeks to gain unauthorized access to computer systems.

Head crash: a catastrophic malfunction in a hard-disk drive, during which the electronic read/write head touches the rapidly spinning disk, gouging its magnetic surface and destroying both its data and the head.

Hot site: a backup facility equipped with functioning computers.

Key: a sequence of symbols used to encrypt and decrypt data.

Key-distribution center: a communications facility in a single-key encryption network that translates a session key encrypted by a message sender into one encrypted with the recipient's key, allowing secure electronic transmission of keys.

Logic bomb: malicious action, initiated by software, that takes effect only when specified conditions occur. Logic bombs often delete data or inhibit normal system functions.

Magnetic tape: plastic tape coated with a magnetic material that stores information in the form of magnetized particles.

Mantrap: a booth between an unsecured area and a secure area such as a computer facility that consists of a pair of electronically controlled doors; the door to the secure area opens only when the user has passed an identity test and the other door has locked.

Message Authentication Code (MAC): a component of the Data Encryption Standard (DES) used to ensure that a message has not been altered.

Modem: a modulator/demodulator device that enables data to be transmitted between computers, generally over telephone lines but sometimes on fiber-optic cable or radio frequencies.

Motor-generator set: an electric motor that drives an electrical generator, which in turn supplies stable power to a mainframe computer, guarding against voltage transients.

Multiplexer: a circuit that transmits several signals simultaneously on a single output channel or wire; *see also* demultiplexer.

One-time pad: a cipher system that uses a notepad of separate ciphers that represent each character of a message as a long series of randomly selected digits. Sender and receiver possess identical pads; each cipher is used only once, then destroyed.

Operating system: a complex set of programs that controls, assists and supervises all other programs run on a computer.

Parity: a bit that indicates whether the number of ones in a bit string is odd or even.

Password: a user's secret sequence of keyboard characters, which must be entered at the beginning of each computer session to verify the user's identity.

Permutation: encrypting data or messages by rearranging the order of their characters; also known as transposition.

Phone phreaking: electronically manipulating telephone signals to deceive billing computers and thus avoid paying for long-distance calls.

Piggybacking: gaining illicit access to a computer facility by following an authorized employee through a controlled door; also known as tailgating.

Plaintext: intelligible text or signals that do not require decryption.

Port: the connection between a computer and another device through which data enters and leaves.

Port protection device (PPD): a microprocessor-driven box that answers a telephone and requires a valid password before connecting a caller to the computer.

Public-key system: a cipher that usually employs a pair of mathematically related keys, one that is public knowledge within the computer network, the other known only to its owner. The sender uses the receiver's public key to encrypt data, which may be decrypted only with the related private key.

Read-access: a user's authorization to view information stored in a computer file.

Reference monitor: a tamperproof operating-system program that classifies users and files, checks each access attempt for proper authorization and denies access to unauthorized users.

Risk analysis: a mathematical method that is used to rank physical and human threats to computers and to their programs and data.

RSA system: a public-key cipher for commercial data that is based on the products of prime numbers; the initials stand for Rivest, Shamir and Adleman, the system's designers.

Scavenging: randomly searching for valuable data in a computer's memory or in discarded or incompletely erased magnetic disks and tapes.

Secret key: a recipient's private key in a public-key system.

Sector: a defined portion of a concentric track on a magnetic disk.

Security filter: a set of software programs that prevents data from being transmitted to unauthorized users or over unprotected communications links.

Session key: the key used to encrypt a single message; *see* key-distribution center.

Single-key system: a cipher that encrypts and decrypts data with the same key.

Software: instructions, or programs, designed to be carried out by a computer.

Substitution: a method for encrypting text or data by substituting different characters for the original ones.

Surge suppressor: a protective electronic circuit for desktop computers that damps voltage transients.

Terminal: a device composed of a keyboard for putting data into a computer and a video screen or printer for receiving data from the computer.

Time bomb: an unauthorized program that takes effect on a specified future date, usually for a hostile purpose.

Time sharing: the simultaneous use of a computer by more than one person in a multi-user network.

Track: a concentric band on a magnetic disk that contains a specified amount of data.

Transducer: a device that converts one type of energy to another.

Transients: momentary, destructive fluctuations in the voltage supplied to a computer.

Transmitter: a device that sends data over a communications link; also, a device that translates electronic signals into electromagnetic waves.

Transposition: *see* permutation.

Trap door: a set of special instructions, usually written by software developers to simplify troubleshooting, that bypasses security procedures and allows direct access to a computer's operating system or to other software.

Trojan horse: a program, purporting to be legitimate, that conceals instructions to breach security whenever the software is invoked.

Uninterruptible power supply (UPS): a complex network of electronic circuitry and storage batteries that filters out transients and provides virtually instantaneous backup power in case of blackout.

Virus: a set of instructions, often malicious, that can spread from computer to computer by attaching to otherwise legitimate programs.

Voltage: a measure of the force that causes electrical current to flow through a circuit.

Wiretapping: monitoring or recording data as it moves across a communications link.

Work factor: an estimate of the time or effort needed to break a code, cipher or other security measure.

Worm: a program that disperses copies of itself throughout a computer system or network.

Write-access: a user's authorization to record or alter data stored in a computer.

The Language of Bits

When confidential data is encrypted for transmission or storage (*pages 103-117*), both the data and the key used to encode it are converted to strings of bits, the binary digits one and zero, which represent the on-off electronic pulses that are a computer's real language. Depending on what the machine has been programmed to expect, the same sequence of zeros and ones—1000001, say—may represent the decimal value 65 or the roman letter A. (A similar string may represent neither a number nor a letter but instead be an instruction to the computer to add or subtract; a series of such strings could tell the computer to color the screen red.)

At far left is a table listing the binary number system's seven-bit equivalents for the decimal values 0 through 127. As illustrated in the small tables at near left, the value of a binary digit is determined by where it stands in relation to other digits in the string, just as in the decimal system.

Although the binary equivalents of decimal numbers are mathematically based, the binary codes for the characters on a keyboard are arbitrary. In theory, any string of ones and zeros could represent a character; in practice, standard representations have been devised to enable computers to perform useful operations such as alphabetizing. The convention also allows computers to communicate electronically with one another and with a variety of peripheral devices, such as keyboards and printers. At near left is a partial list of the binary code for alphabetic and numeric characters as established by the American Standard Code for Information Interchange (ASCII). ASCII assigns a string of seven bits—plus another bit for checking purposes (*below*)—to each upper- and lower-case letter of the alphabet, to the 10 decimal symbols, and to punctuation marks and control characters (for keyboard or printer functions, such as carriage return or backspace). ASCII is the most widely used convention in the United States; other countries employ modified international versions.

Decimal place values

PLACE 100	PLACE 10	PLACE 1
1	0	9

In a decimal number, each column to the left increases in value by the power of 10: 1, 10, 100, 1,000 and so on. An individual number is the sum of the values of its place columns. Here, one 100, no 10s and nine 1s equals 109.

$$100 + 0 + 9 = 109$$

Binary place values

PLACE 64	PLACE 32	PLACE 16	PLACE 8	PLACE 4	PLACE 2	PLACE 1
1	1	0	1	1	0	1

In binary, the value of each column to the left increases by the power of two: 1, 2, 4 and so on. Only two symbols, 1 and 0, mark place values. Here, one 64, one 32, no 16s, one 8, one 4, no 2s and one 1 combine to equal 109.

$$64 + 32 + 0 + 8 + 4 + 0 + 1 = 109$$

DECIMAL NUMBER / BINARY EQUIVALENT

DECIMAL (100 10 1)	64	32	16	8	4	2	1
0	0	0	0	0	0	0	0
1	0	0	0	0	0	0	1
2	0	0	0	0	0	1	0
3	0	0	0	0	0	1	1
4	0	0	0	0	1	0	0
5	0	0	0	0	1	0	1
6	0	0	0	0	1	1	0
7	0	0	0	0	1	1	1
8	0	0	0	1	0	0	0
9	0	0	0	1	0	0	1
10	0	0	0	1	0	1	0
11	0	0	0	1	0	1	1
12	0	0	0	1	1	0	0
13	0	0	0	1	1	0	1
14	0	0	0	1	1	1	0
15	0	0	0	1	1	1	1
16	0	0	1	0	0	0	0
17	0	0	1	0	0	0	1
18	0	0	1	0	0	1	0
19	0	0	1	0	0	1	1
20	0	0	1	0	1	0	0
21	0	0	1	0	1	0	1
22	0	0	1	0	1	1	0
23	0	0	1	0	1	1	1
24	0	0	1	1	0	0	0
25	0	0	1	1	0	0	1
26	0	0	1	1	0	1	0
27	0	0	1	1	0	1	1
28	0	0	1	1	1	0	0
29	0	0	1	1	1	0	1
30	0	0	1	1	1	1	0
31	0	0	1	1	1	1	1
32	0	1	0	0	0	0	0
33	0	1	0	0	0	0	1
34	0	1	0	0	0	1	0
35	0	1	0	0	0	1	1
36	0	1	0	0	1	0	0
37	0	1	0	0	1	0	1
38	0	1	0	0	1	1	0
39	0	1	0	0	1	1	1
40	0	1	0	1	0	0	0
41	0	1	0	1	0	0	1
42	0	1	0	1	0	1	0
43	0	1	0	1	0	1	1
44	0	1	0	1	1	0	0
45	0	1	0	1	1	0	1
46	0	1	0	1	1	1	0
47	0	1	0	1	1	1	1
48	0	1	1	0	0	0	0
49	0	1	1	0	0	0	1
50	0	1	1	0	0	1	0
51	0	1	1	0	0	1	1
52	0	1	1	0	1	0	0
53	0	1	1	0	1	0	1
54	0	1	1	0	1	1	0
55	0	1	1	0	1	1	1
56	0	1	1	1	0	0	0
57	0	1	1	1	0	0	1
58	0	1	1	1	0	1	0
59	0	1	1	1	0	1	1
60	0	1	1	1	1	0	0
61	0	1	1	1	1	0	1

ASCII CODE

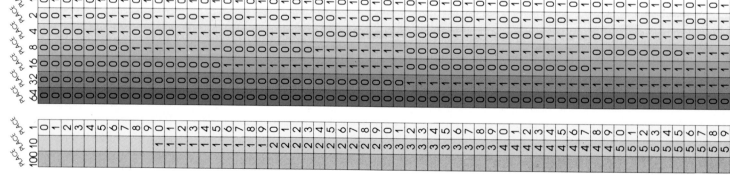

(space)	0	1	0	0	0	0	0	0
!	0	1	0	0	0	0	0	1
"	0	1	0	0	0	0	1	0
#	0	1	0	0	0	0	1	1
$	0	1	0	0	0	1	0	0
%	0	1	0	0	0	1	0	1
&	0	1	0	0	0	1	1	0
'	0	1	0	0	0	1	1	1
(	0	1	0	0	1	0	0	0
)	0	1	0	0	1	0	0	1
*	0	1	0	0	1	0	1	0
+	0	1	0	0	1	0	1	1
,	0	1	0	0	1	1	0	0
-	0	1	0	0	1	1	0	1
.	0	1	0	0	1	1	1	0
/	0	1	0	0	1	1	1	1
0	0	1	0	1	0	0	0	0
1	0	1	0	1	0	0	0	1
2	0	1	0	1	0	0	1	0
3	0	1	0	1	0	0	1	1
4	0	1	0	1	0	1	0	0
5	0	1	0	1	0	1	0	1
6	0	1	0	1	0	1	1	0
7	0	1	0	1	0	1	1	1
8	0	1	0	1	1	0	0	0
9	0	1	0	1	1	0	0	1
: ;	0	1	0	1	1	0	1	0
<	0	1	0	1	1	1	0	0

At far left are the 128 possible combinations of one and zero in a seven-bit string—the equivalents of the decimal numbers 0 through 127. At near left, starting with the binary equivalent of 32, are 96 of the same strings as they are used in ASCII to designate keyboard characters. The ASCII list actually begins with 32 codes for control functions, such as carriage return and backspace; it ends with a code for the delete function.

An Extra Bit for Parity

In addition to the seven bits used to encode binary numbers and ASCII characters, each string may have an extra bit space, normally reserved for a checking mechanism known as a parity bit. A parity bit is like a flag that signals whether errors have occurred during the transmission of data from one computer to another. A computer transmits data in either odd or even parity. Odd parity means that each bit string must have an odd number of ones; during transmission, the computer places either a one or a zero in the string's unused bit space to make the total number of ones odd. The receiving computer then checks to see if the number of ones it receives matches the message's parity designation. Usually the leftmost bit space is reserved for a parity bit, as with the ASCII code for B, below. In rare cases, as with the Data Encryption Standard key on page 108, the rightmost space is used; in the example at bottom, the binary equivalent of the decimal number one is followed by an extra zero for odd parity.

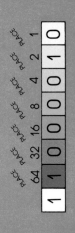

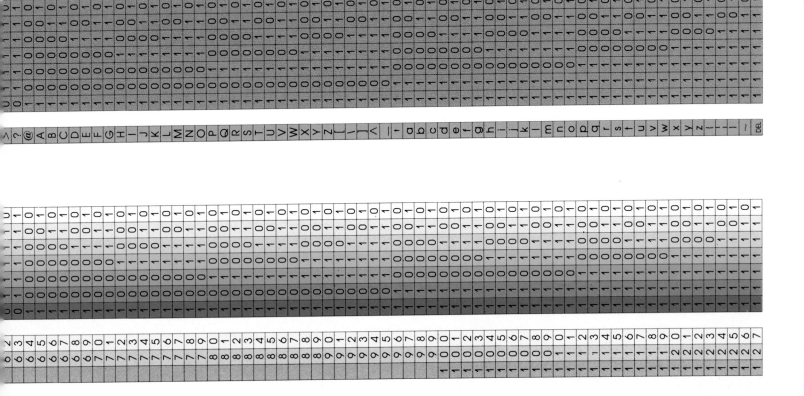

Bibliography

Books

Beker, Henry, and Fred Piper, *Cipher Systems*. New York: John Wiley and Sons, 1982.

Bosworth, Bruce, *Codes, Ciphers, and Computers*. New York: Hayden Book Company, Inc., 1982.

Burnham, David, *The Rise of the Computer State*. New York: Random House, 1983.

Castleman, Kenneth R., *Digital Image Processing*. Englewood Cliffs, N.J.: Prentice-Hall, 1979.

Computer Piracy and Privacy (Home of the Future: Industry Research Report series). Boston: The Yankee Group, 1984.

Cooper, James Arlin, *Computer-Security Technology*. Lexington, Mass.: Lexington Books, 1984.

Davies, D. W., and W. L. Price, *Security for Computer Networks*. New York: John Wiley & Sons, 1984.

Deavours, Cipher A., and Louis Kruh, *Machine Cryptography and Modern Cryptanalysis*. Dedham, Mass.: Artech House, 1985.

The Electronic Vault: Computer Piracy and Privacy (Home of the Future: Industry Research Report series). Boston: The Yankee Group, 1984.

Fike, John L., and George E. Friend, *Understanding Telephone Electronics*. Dallas, Tex.: Texas Instruments Incorporated, 1983.

Hemphill, Charles F., Jr., and Robert D. Hemphill, *Security Safeguards for the Computer*. New York: AMACOM, 1979.

Hsiao, David K., Douglas S. Kerr and Stuart E. Madnick, *Computer Security*. New York: Academic Press, 1979.

Kahn, David:
   The Codebreakers. New York: Macmillan Company, 1967.
   Kahn on Codes. New York: Macmillan Company, 1983.

Katzen, Harry, Jr., *The Standard Data Encryption Algorithm*. New York: Petrocelli Books, 1977.

Lavington, Simon, *Early British Computers*. Manchester, England: Manchester University Press, 1980.

Lewin, Ronald, *Ultra Goes to War*. New York: McGraw-Hill, 1978.

Metropolis, N., J. Howlett and Gian-Carlo Rota, eds., *A History of Computing in the Twentieth Century: A Collection of Essays*. New York: Academic Press, 1980.

Meyer, Carl H., and Stephen M. Matyas, *Cryptography: A New Dimension in Computer Data Security*. New York: John Wiley & Sons, 1982.

Norman, Adrian R. D., *Computer Insecurity*. London: Chapman and Hall, 1983.

Parker, Donn B.:
   Crime by Computer. New York: Charles Scribner's Sons, 1976.
   Fighting Computer Crime. New York: Charles Scribner's Sons, 1983.

Shurkin, Joel, *Engines of the Mind*. New York: W. W. Norton & Company, 1984.

Troy, Eugene F., Stuart W. Katzke and Dennis D. Steinauer, *Technical Solutions to the Computer Security Intrusion Problem*. Washington, D.C.: National Science Foundation, 1984.

Turn, Rein, ed., *Advances in Computer System Security*. Vol. 2. Dedham, Mass.: Artech House, 1984.

Welchman, Gordon, *Breaking the Enigma Codes*. New York: McGraw-Hill, 1982.

Whiteside, Thomas, *Computer Capers*. New York: Thomas Y. Crowell Company, 1978.

Zaks, Rodnay, and Austin Lesea, *Microprocessor Interfacing Techniques*. Berkeley, Calif.: Sybex, 1979.

Periodicals

Baird, Lindsay L., "Sensible Network Security." *Datamation*, February 1, 1985.

Beker, Henry, and Fred Piper, "Cryptography for Beginners." *New Scientist*, July 1983.

Bernhard, Robert, "Breaching System Security." *IEEE Spectrum*, June 1982.

"Biometric Security Systems." *Data Processing & Communications Security*, Vol. 8, No. 6, no date.

Block, David, "The Trapdoor Algorithm." *Creative Computing*, May 1983.

Boebert, W. E., R. Y. Kain and W. D. Young, "Secure Computing: The Secure Ada Target Approach." *Scientific Honeyweller*, July 1985.

Browne, Malcolm W., "Locking Out the Hackers." *Discover*, November 1983.

Cannon, T. M., and B. R. Hunt, "Image Processing by Computer." *Scientific American*, October 1981.

Chenoweth, Karin, "Libraries Survive the Ides of March." *The Montgomery Journal* (Montgomery County, Md.), March 18, 1982.

Cohen, Laurie P., "Internal Security." *The Wall Street Journal*, September 16, 1985.

Colby, Wendelin, "Burnt or Burned." *Infosystems*, February 1985.

Cook, Rick, "Power Line Protection." *Popular Computing*, November 1984.

"Cracking Down on Crime." *Datamation*, May 1, 1985.

Dewdney, A. K., "Computer Recreations." *Scientific American*, September 1985.

DiNucci, Darcy, "Copying Software: Who's Right?" *PC World*, Vol. 3, Issue 9, no date.

Downs, Deborah D., "Operating Systems Key Security with Basic Software Mechanisms." *Electronics*, March 8, 1984.

Edersheim, Peggy, "Computer Crime." *The Wall Street Journal*, August 15, 1985.

Elmer-Dewitt, Philip, "Invasion of the Data Snatchers." *Time*, September 26, 1988.

Flowers, Thomas H., "The Design of Colossus." *Annals of the History of Computing*, July 1983.

Gillard, Collen, and Jim Smith, "Computer Crime: A Growing Threat." *BYTE*, October 1983.

Gorney, Cynthia, "Hack Attack." *The Washington Post*, December 6, 1984.

Hellman, Martin E., "The Mathematics of Public-Key Cryptography." *Scientific American*, August 1979.

"His Master's (Digital) Voice." *Time*, April 1, 1985.

Horgan, John, "Thwarting the Information Thieves." *IEEE Spectrum*, July 1985.

Howitt, Doran, "Of Worms and Booby Traps." *InfoWorld*, November 19, 1984.

Immel, A. Richard, "Data Security." *Popular Computing*, May 1984.

"Innovations: Patents, Processes, and Products." *IEEE Spectrum*, October 1985.

Janulartis, Victor:

"Creating a Disaster Recovery Plan." *Infosystems,* February 1985.

"Getting a Grip on Disaster Planning Needs." *Infosystems,* February 1985.

"Key Proposal: ADAPSO Seeks a Hardware Solution to Piracy." *Business Computer Systems,* February 1985.

Kolata, Gina:

"Computer Break-Ins Fan Security Fears." *Science,* September 2, 1983.

"Scheme to Foil Software Pirates." *Science,* September 23, 1983.

"When Criminals Turn to Computers, Is Anything Safe?" *Smithsonian,* August 1982.

Larson, Harry T., "Who Goes There?" *Hardcopy,* March 1985.

Leadabrand, Russ, "Thwarting Computer Thieves." *Computer Merchandising,* November 1983.

McAfee, John, "The Virus Cure." *Datamation,* February 15, 1989.

McLellen, Vin, "Phone Phink: A Super-Hacker Turns State's Evidence." *Digital Review,* January 1985.

Mager, Gary, "Saving Your Computer from Surges, Sags or Noise." *The DEC Professional,* December 1984.

Marbach, William D., et al., "Beware: Hackers at Play." *Newsweek,* September 5, 1983.

Markoff, John, Phillip Robinson and Ezra Shapiro, "Up to Date." *BYTE,* March 1985.

Maude, Tim, and Derwent Maude, "Hardware Protection against Software Piracy." *Communications of the ACM,* September 1984.

Murphy, Jamie, "A Threat from Malicious Software." *Time,* November 4, 1985.

Myers, Edith, "Speaking in Codes." *Datamation,* December 1, 1984.

"New Code Is Broken." *Science,* May 1982.

Ognibene, Peter J.:

"Computer Saboteurs." *Science Digest,* July 1984.

"Secret Ciphers Solved: Artificial Intelligence." *OMNI,* November 1984.

Rapoport, Roger, "Unbreakable Code." *OMNI,* September 1980.

Rosch, Winn L., "PC Data Is Vulnerable to Attack." *PC Magazine,* July 23, 1985.

Sandza, Richard, "The Night of the Hackers." *Newsweek,* November 12, 1984.

Schlosberg, Jeremy, "Out of Site." *Digital Review,* March 1985.

Schoch, John, and Jon Hupp, "The 'Worm' Programs." *Communications of the ACM,* March 1982.

Schrager, Barry, "Outwitting 2-Bit Thieves and Arresting Computer Crime." *Data Communications,* November 1982.

"Security and Vax/VMS." *The DEC Professional,* December 1984.

Shannon, Terry C., "Computer Security—a Checklist." *The DEC Professional,* December 1984.

Small, David, "The Futility of Copy Protection." *Tech Journal,* December 1985.

Smiddy, James D., and Linda O. Smiddy, "Caught in the Act." *Datamation,* June 15, 1985.

Smith, Jim:

"Call-Back Schemes Ward Off Unwanted Access by Telephone." *Electronics,* March 8, 1984.

"Callback Security System Prevents Unauthorized Computer Access." *Mini-Micro Systems,* July 1984.

Solomon, Les, and Stan Veit, "Data Storage in a Nutshell." *Computers & Electronics,* July 1983.

"The Spreading Danger of Computer Crime." *Business Week,* April 20, 1981.

Sullivan, Joseph, "Cryptography: Securing Computer Transmissions." *High Technology,* November 1983.

"Taking a Byte out of Crime." *Time,* October 14, 1985.

Thé, Lee, "Controlling Access to Your Data." *Personal Computing,* September 1985.

Thornton, Mary, " 'Hackers' Ignore Consequences of Their High-Tech Joy Rides." *The Washington Post,* May 2, 1984.

"A Threat from Malicious Software." *Time,* November 4, 1985.

Troy, Gene, "Thwarting the Hackers: New Security Protection Devices." *Datamation,* July 1, 1984.

Tubb, Phillip, "A Layman's Guide to Disk Protection." *Creative Computing,* July 1983.

"Vault Delays 'Worm' Plan." *InfoWorld,* January 21, 1985.

Wellborn, Stanley N., "Foolproof ID: Opening Locks with Your Body." *U.S. News & World Report,* December 17, 1984.

Wong, Kenneth, "Computer Disaster in the United Kingdom." *Edpacs,* January 1985.

Zimmerman, Joel, "Is Your Computer Insecure?" *Datamation,* May 15, 1985.

Other Publications

Barton, Ben F., and Marthalee S. Barton, "User-Friendly Password Methods for Computer-Mediated Information Systems." *Computers & Security 3,* Amsterdam, the Netherlands: Elsevier Science Publishers B. V., 1984.

Branstad, Dennis K., and Miles E. Smid, "Integrity and Security Standards Based on Cryptography." *Computers & Security 1,* Amsterdam, the Netherlands: Elsevier Science Publishers B. V., 1982.

Cohen, Fred, "Computer Viruses: Theory and Experiments." 7th DOD/NBS Computer Security Conference, September 1984.

Colvin, Bill D., "Computer Crime Investigators: A New Training Field." *FBI Law Enforcement Bulletin,* July 1979.

"Computer Crime." *Criminal Justice Resource Manual.* Washington, D.C.: Bureau of Justice Statistics/U.S. Department of Justice, 1979.

"Data Encryption Standard." *Federal Information Processing Standards Publication 46.* Washington, D.C.: U.S. Department of Commerce/National Bureau of Standards, January 15, 1977.

Eisenberg, Ted, David Gries, Juris Hartmanis et al., *The Computer Worm: A Report to the Provost.* Ithaca, New York: Cornell University, February 6, 1989.

"The EyeDentification System 7.5: Health, Safety and Statistical Performance Review." Beaverton, Ore.: EyeDentify, Inc., December 1984.

"Guidelines for Automatic Data Processing Physical Security and Risk Management." *Federal Information Processing Standards Publication 31.* Washington, D.C.: U.S. Department of Commerce/National Bureau of Standards, June 1974.

"Guidelines for Implementing and Using the NBS Data Encryption Standard." *Federal Information Processing Standards Publication 74.* Washington, D.C.: U.S. Department of Commerce/

National Bureau of Standards, April 1, 1981.

"Guidelines on Evaluation of Techniques for Automated Personal Identification." *Federal Information Processing Standards Publication 48.* Washington, D.C.: U.S. Department of Commerce/ National Bureau of Standards, April 1, 1977.

"Guidelines on User Authentication Techniques for Computer Network Access Control." *Federal Information Processing Standards Publication 83.* Washington, D.C.: U.S. Department of Commerce/National Bureau of Standards, September 1980.

Henkel, Tom, and Peter Bartolik, eds., "Protecting the Corporate Data Resource." Special Report, *Computerworld,* November 28, 1983.

Herschberg, I. S., and R. Paans, "The Programmer's Threat: Cases and Causes." *Computers & Security 3.* Amsterdam, the Netherlands: Elsevier Science Publishers B. V., 1984.

Murray, William H., "Computer Security: Observations on the State of the Technology." *Computers & Security 2,* Amsterdam, the Netherlands: Elsevier Science Publishers B. V., 1983.

Sanders, C. W., et al., *Study of Vulnerability of Electronic Communication Systems to Electronic Interception.* McLean, Va.: The Mitre Corporation, January 1977.

Schell, Roger R., "Computer Security: The Achilles' Heel of the Electronic Air Force?" *Air University Review,* January-February 1979.

"Security of Personal Computer Systems: A Management Guide." *NBS Special Publication 500-120,* Institute for Computer Sciences and Technology, National Bureau of Standards, no date.

Smid, Miles E., "Integrating the Data Encryption Standard into Computer Networks." *IEEE Transactions on Communications,* June 1981.

Steinauer, Dennis D., *Security of Personal Computers: A Growing Concern.* Washington, D.C.: National Bureau of Standards, no date.

Stokes, Robert S., "Scam-Free S.W.I.F.T. Net May Not Be 'Sting'-Proof." *Management Information Systems Week,* Vol. 3, No. 28, no date.

Tangney, John D., "History of Protection in Computer Systems." *MITRE Technical Report.* The Mitre Corporation, 1981.

Thompson, Phil, Alan Silver and Michael Brown, *Copy II Plus.* Portland, Ore.: Central Point Software, Inc., no date.

Troy, Eugene F., "Dial-Up Security Update." *Proceedings of the 8th National Computer Security Conference.* Gaithersburg, Md., September-October 1985.

Troy, Eugene F., Stuart W. Katzke and Dennis D. Steinauer, *Technical Solutions to the Computer Security Intrusion Problem.* Washington, D.C.: National Bureau of Standards, November 2, 1984.

Turn, Rein, "Private Sector Needs for Trusted/Secure Computer Systems." *Report R-2811-DR&E Trusted Computer Systems: Needs and Incentives for Use in Government and the Private Sector.* The Rand Corporation, June 1981.

Wood, Helen M., *Computer Science & Technology: The Use of Passwords for Controlled Access to Computer Resources.* Washington, D.C.: Institute for Computer Sciences and Technology, National Bureau of Standards, May 1977.

Worthington, T. K., et al., "IBM Dynamic Signature Verification." *Computer Security.* Amsterdam, the Netherlands: Elsevier Science Publishers B. V., 1985.

Acknowledgments

The index for this book was prepared by Mel Ingber. The editors also wish to thank: California—Carlsbad: Helen C. Remington, Allenbach Industries; Menlo Park: Donn Parker, SRI International; Mountainview: Robert B. Barnes, Drexler Technology Corporation; Whitfield Diffie, Bell Northern Research Incorporated; Palo Alto: Randall Hawks, Identix Incorporated; Redwood City: D. James Bidzos, RSA Data Security; San Jose: Alan H. Keating, Stellar Systems; Colorado—Colorado Springs: Virginia Sullivan, North American Aerospace Defense Command; Maryland—Fort Meade: Marvin Schaefer, National Computer Security Center; Gaithersburg: David Balenson, National Bureau of Standards; Owings Mills: John Hynes, Malco Security Magnetics; Massachusetts—Arlington: Ronald Rivest; Cambridge: Daniel Sevush, Lotus Development Corporation; Weston: Eric Newhouse; New Mexico—Albuquerque: Russell Maxwell; New York—Yorktown Heights: Thomas Worthington, IBM Corporation; Ohio—Columbus: David Schinke, AT&T Bell Laboratories; Oregon—Portland: Michael Brown, Central Point Software; Steven Flego, EyeDentify, Inc.; Pennsylvania—Philadelphia: Ian Murphy, Secure Data Systems; Texas—Dallas: George Doddington, Texas Instruments.

Picture Credits

The sources for the illustrations that appear in this book are listed below. Credits from left to right are separated by semicolons, from top to bottom by dashes.
Cover, 6: Art by Andrea Baruffi. 12-15: Art by Aaron Bowles. 21-25: Art by Steve Wagner. 26: Art by Andrea Baruffi. 31: Art by William J. Hennessy Jr. 36-39: Art by Peter Sawyer. 43: Art by William J. Hennessy Jr. 45-49: Art by Matt McMullen. 50, 51: Art by Matt McMullen—courtesy AT&T Bell Laboratories. 52-57: Art by Matt McMullen. 58-62: Art by Andrea Baruffi. 65-67: Art by Frederic F. Bigio from B-C Graphics. 70-85: Art by William J. Hennessy Jr. 86-91: Art by Andrea Baruffi. 94-97: Art by Wayne Vincent. 103-117: Art by Sam Haltom.

Index

P

Paans, Ronald, 72
Parker, Donn, 17
Passwords, 9, 21, *22-25*, 70-71; circumventing, 71
Permutation, 88, 104, *105*
Phone phreaks, 16
Physical attacks on computer systems, 35, 42, 44. *See also* Terrorist attacks on computer systems
Physical defenses, 41
Piggybacking, 41
Plaintext, 104
Poe, Edgar Allan, 89
Port protection device (PPD), 71; circumventing, 71
Power supply, auxiliary, 32-33
Power-supply problems, 30-33
Printers, and security, *12*
Programmers, as security threats, 72. *See also* Employee attacks on computer systems
Public-key systems, 99-102, 103, *112-117*; digital signature, 101-102, *116-117*; RSA, 101-102, 103; trap-door knapsack, 99-101

R

Red Brigade, 35
Reference monitor, 72, 73, *82-85*
Retinal-identification system, *52-53*
Rifkin, Stanley, 17
Risk analysis, 28-29
Rivest, Ronald, 101, 112
RSA system, 101-102, *112-117*

S

Sabotage, 40
Sandberg-Diment, Eric, 33
Sandza, Richard, 10
Satellite transmission of data, *94, 95, 96-97*
Scherbius, Arthur, 90
Schlüsselzusatz, 91-92
Schneider, Jerry Neal, 63
Schoch, John, 68
Scores virus, 69
Scytale, 88
Security systems, 11; business of, 11, 16; cost, 20, 42. *See also specific systems*
Shamir, Adi, 100, 112
Signature, digital, *116-117*
Signature-identification system, *48-49*
Smart card, *30-31*
Software piracy, 64. *See also* Copy protection
Stallman, Richard, 11
Static electricity, 29-30
Streeter, Richard, 59
Substitution, *104*
Surge suppressors, 32
Surveillance devices, 41
S.W.I.F.T. (Society for Worldwide Interbank Financial Telecommunications), 87

T

Telephone system, manipulation of, 16
Terminals, and access to computers, *12, 13*

Terrorist attacks on computer systems, 35, 40, 41, 42; in Italy, 40; in Japan, 40; in United States, 35
Texas Instruments, *43*
Time bomb, 14
Time sharing, 9, 72, 92
Transients, electrical, 30-32
Trap door, 14, 63-65
Trap-door problem, and encryption, 100-101
Trojan horses, 18-19, 59, 60, 64-68, *78-81*, 85
Turing, Alan, 91

U

Ultra, 91
Uninterruptible power supply (UPS), 32-33; personal computers, 33

V

Viruses, 18, 19, 69
Voice-identification systems, 43, *50-51*
Voltage regulators, 32

W

WarGames, 64
Water hazards, 33
Watermark magnetics, *30-31*
Work factor, 90
Worms, 68

Z

Zimmerman, Joel S., 28

TIME-LIFE BOOKS

EDITOR-IN-CHIEF: Thomas H. Flaherty

Director of Editorial Resources: Elise D. Ritter-Clough
Executive Art Director: Ellen Robling
Director of Photography and Research:
John Conrad Weiser
Editorial Board: Dale M. Brown, Janet Cave,
Roberta Conlan, Robert Doyle, Laura Foreman,
Jim Hicks, Rita Thievon Mullin, Henry Woodhead
Assistant Director of Editorial Resources:
Norma E. Shaw

PRESIDENT: John D. Hall

Vice President and Director of Marketing:
Nancy K. Jones
Editorial Director: Lee Hassig
Director of Production Services: Robert N. Carr
Production Manager: Marlene Zack
Director of Technology: Eileen Bradley
Supervisor of Quality Control: James King

Editorial Operations
Production: Celia Beattie
Library: Louise D. Forstall
Computer Composition: Deborah G. Tait (Manager),
Monika D. Thayer, Janet Barnes Syring, Lillian Daniels
Interactive Media Specialist: Patti H. Cass

Time-Life Books is a division of
Time Life Incorporated

PRESIDENT AND CEO: John M. Fahey, Jr.

Correspondents: Elisabeth Kraemer-Singh (Bonn),
Christina Lieberman (New York); Maria Vincenza
Aloisi (Paris); Ann Natanson (Rome). Valuable assistance was also provided by Marlin Levin (Jerusalem).

UNDERSTANDING COMPUTERS

SERIES DIRECTOR: Roberta Conlan
Series Administrator: Rita Thievon Mullin

Editorial Staff for *Computer Security*
Designer: Ellen Robling
Associate Editors: Lee Hassig (text),
Judith W. Shanks (pictures)
Researchers: Roxie France-Nuriddin,
Tina S. McDowell
Writer: Lydia Preston
Assistant Designer: Antonio Alcalá
Copy Coordinators: Anthony K. Pordes,
Jayne E. Rohrich, Robert M. S. Somerville
Picture Coordinator: Renée DeSandies
Editorial Assistant: Miriam Newton Morrison

Special Contributors: (text) Ronald H. Bailey, Sarah
Brash, Richard D. James, John I. Merritt, Charles C.
Smith, David Thiemann; (research) Pamela Colbert,
Isabel Fucigna, Sara Mark

GENERAL CONSULTANT

ISABEL LIDA NIRENBERG has dealt with a wide range of computer applications, from the analysis of data collected by the Pioneer space probes to the matching of children and families for adoption agencies. She works at the Computer Center at the State University of New York at Albany, and assists faculty and students there with microcomputer applications.

OTHER CONSULTANTS

DR. DENNIS BRANSTAD is a National Bureau of Standards Computer Science Fellow in computer security in the Institute for Computer Sciences and Technology. He has been responsible for the development of computer-security standards for the government and private industry since 1973.

JAMES ARLIN COOPER works at the Sandia National Laboratories in Albuquerque, New Mexico, and is also an Adjunct Professor of Electrical Engineering at the University of New Mexico.

DR. STUART KATZKE heads the Computer Security Management and Evaluation Group in the Institute for Computer Sciences and Technology at the National Bureau of Standards. He is responsible for the development of federal information-processing standards and computer-security guidelines.

CARL E. LANDWEHR is a computer scientist at the Naval Research Laboratory. The author of several articles on computer security, he has also served on the computer-science faculties of Purdue and Georgetown universities.

CATHERINE MEADOWS is a mathematician at the Naval Research Laboratory and a specialist in computer cryptography who has published several papers on the subject.

JAMES ROSS owns Ross Engineering, Inc., a company that specializes in devising countermeasures to computer crime and technical surveillance. He has also taught electronics at West Point and at Capitol Institute of Technology in Maryland.

MILES SMID is manager of the Security and Speech Technology Group in the Institute for Computer Sciences and Technology at the National Bureau of Standards. He is a major contributor to the electronic funds transfer security standards adopted by the U.S. Department of Treasury and the American Banking Association.

Library of Congress Cataloging in Publication Data

Main entry under title:
Computer security / by the editors of Time-Life Books.
    p.   cm. (Understanding computers)
Includes bibliographical references
    1. Computers—Access control. I. Time-Life Books.
II. Series.
QA76.9.A25C635 1990   005.8—dc20   89-20428
ISBN 0-8094-7566-9
ISBN 0-8094-7567-7 (lib. bdg.)

REVISIONS STAFF

EDITOR: Lee Hassig

Writer: Esther Ferington
Assistant Designer: Tina Taylor
Copy Coordinator: Anne Farr
Picture Coordinator: Katherine Griffin

Consultants:
Dennis Branstad (see OTHER CONSULTANTS).

Damian Saccocio is interested in issues of technology and policy related to computer science. He works for the Computer Science and Technology Board of the National Academy of Sciences.

Eugene Spafford, a member of the Purdue University Computer Sciences Department, specializes in the area of computer system fallibility. He is also concerned with issues of computer ethics, education and professionalism.